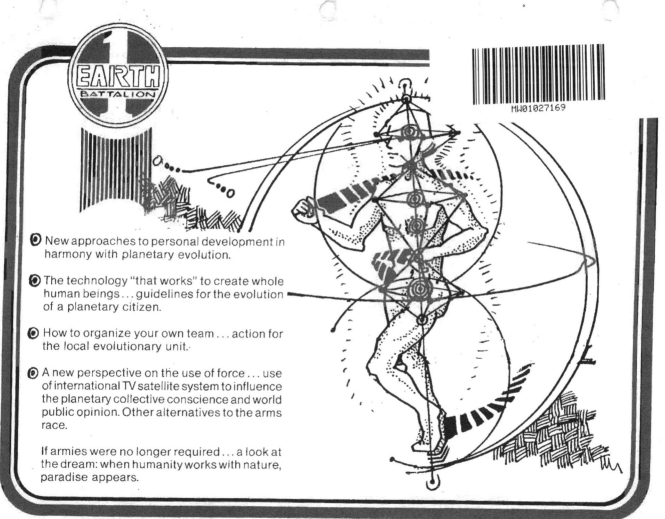

1 EARTH BATTALION

- New approaches to personal development in harmony with planetary evolution.

- The technology "that works" to create whole human beings . . . guidelines for the evolution of a planetary citizen.

- How to organize your own team . . . action for the local evolutionary unit.

- A new perspective on the use of force . . . use of international TV satellite system to influence the planetary collective conscience and world public opinion. Other alternatives to the arms race.

  If armies were no longer required . . . a look at the dream: when humanity works with nature, paradise appears.

THE FIRST EARTH BATTALION

the warrior monk's vision
by Lt. Col Jim Channon, US Army

I envision an international ideal of service awakening in an emerging class of people who are best called *evolutionaries*. I see them as soldiers, as youth, and as those who have soldier spirit within them. I see them come together in the name of *people* and *planet* to create a new environment of support for the positive growth of humankind and the living earth mother. Their mission is to protect the possible and nurture the potential. They are the evolutionary guardians who focus their loving protection and affirm their allegiance to people and planet for their own good and for the good of those they serve. I call them *evolutionaries*, not *revolutionaries*, for they are potentialists, not pragmatists. They are pioneers, not palace guards.

As their contribution to a hopeful future, the warrior monks bring evolutionary tactics. They recognize that the world community of peoples demands hope from those who would operate as servants of the people. Services rendered by the warriors of the First Earth Battalion are specifically designed to generate workable solutions to defuse the nuclear time bomb, promote international relations, spread wise energy use, enforce the ecological balance, assist wise technological expansion, and above all, stress human development.

Armies are both the potential instruments of our destruction and the organized service that can drive humanity's potential development. They are the 'turn key' organizations that could either shift the energy of our world into a positive synergistic convergence, or bring us to the brink of the void. We have no choice but to encourage world armies to accept and express the nobility they already strive to attain. I can see their action expanding to include evolutionary work like planting vast new forests, completing large canal projects, helping in the design and construction of new energy-solvent towns, helping to clean up the inner cities, and working with the troubled inner city youth in young commando groups, and working harmoniously with other nations to see that the plentiful resources of our mother earth are equally shared by all peoples.

This will not be the first time that warrior monks have been active.In Vedic traditions, the warrior monk was a philosopher and teacher, and therefore a powerful transformational player. In the Chinese culture, the warrior was both a healer and teacher of martial arts. History affirms our own belief that there is no contradiction in the warrior and the service oriented monk prototypes living a completely harmonious, blended and parallel path when the basic ethic and service is 'loving protection' of evolution and humankind. There is no contradiction in having armies of the world experience the same ethic as they evolve in peaceful cooperation towards the greater good of all.

THE FIRST EARTH BATTALION

I welcome you to share in the Warrior Monk's vision, and also to share in helping it become a reality. We have no seriously satisfying alternative but to be wonderful.

It is sometimes difficult to determine how we have set ourselves against each other as nations, and even the more frustrating when we realize that the people of these nations are not really very different inside, and in fact have the same desires for growth and environmental balance and for prosperity that we have. But this is reality. And soldiers who have grown up in an 'arms race' world are obviously doing their job of protection when they come up with a new and more effective weapons package. But it is time for another approach, to use all of this military power for another end. It is time to give as much reward for the evolutionary contribution made by a soldier or an army as we have given in the past for the destructive contributions made on behalf of national defense.

I know that this process will begin with the transformation of soldiers and evolutionaries everywhere on the face of our planet home. There are young men and women who already aspire to this level of service and who are ready to make a permanent commitment. They will begin to meet in small groups to provide a support system for the personal transformation of group members. And on a small scale, these groups will begin selected evolutionary programs in their units and their communities. This manual serves as a handbook for the development of these evolutionary players and the development of their operating teams.

All national level armies will begin to cooperate on ventures that stabilize the nuclear balance of terror. Joint teams could then patrol space and counter local terrorist activities that threaten stability in any given areas. Evolved cooperation will stifle the arms race. Cooperation between the Soviets and American military could insure that neither side "flies off the handle" in direct collision in some local arena of tension, which would precipitate both sides into a major nuclear war. And there are precedents for this type of cooperation unknown to the public. The US and Soviet military have partied together in Potsdam. They have exchanged academics at the Staff College level, and they have viewed each other's military exercises in recent years.

The great flow of historical events, habits, and international relations is not easy to change. It will take the patient, focused, loving and dedicated effort of warriors all over the world, people of different languages and cultures and all examples of humanity's infinite variety of expression. What I present in this manual is a small contribution to what surely must be a hope for peace and prosperity that lives in all hearts everywhere. It is not a set system of beliefs and ideas. It is a smorgasbord of new functional ideas. As you respond to these insights, you will be able to adjust them to your own operating style. They should flow into your culture and respond to your country's point of view. Any elaboration on these ideas can then come from your own study. They must work for everyone in some way or they won't really work.

THE FIRST EARTH BATTALION

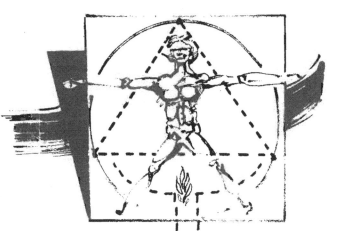

*The earth battalion declares its primary allegiance to **people** and **planet**. You can become a part of that allegiance right where you are simply by allowing the exquisite human being inside to come out. When it's out... help others to come out and then work together cooperatively to stay out — building the paradise that is possible when we cooperate with each other and our mother the earth.*

LEFT BRAIN & RIGHT BRAIN
WORDS & PICTURES

by

Jim Channon LTC. US ARMY
82 © ™

THE IDEAS AND CONCEPTS PRESENTED ARE THOSE OF THE AUTHOR AND HIS CLOSE FRIENDS BOTH IN THE MILITARY AND OUTSIDE. THOUGH MANY OF THE IDEAS ARE NOW SPOKEN ABOUT IN MILITARY CIRCLES THEY DO NOT COMPRISE AN OFFICIAL POSITION BY THE MILITARY AS OF NOW.

THE FIRST EARTH BATTALION

THE FIRST EARTH BATTALION

The First Earth Battalion is a banner under which the forces of good in the world can unite and find strength in spirit with others who share a common goal. Warrior Monks are guardians of the good, guardians of humanity, nature and the planet. Warrior Monks in the United States Army are already teaching soft tactics. Others in the fields of economics, politics, and international affairs are already searching for new ways to work for the greater good in their own arenas. The modern Citizen Samurai in day to day existence is engaged in moral combat to reorganize and focus personal life to its highest good.

This manual was created from the ideas and teachings of over a hundred groups on the New Age Frontier of the West Coast of the United States. It is a primary tool to assist you in giving and getting the most possible from your experience in a human form in the physical realm of this planet earth. It will assist you in preparing for possibilities and events about which you may presently not even be able to dream. Prepare yourself so you will be ready... Begin your work locally until the call goes out for global action.

guidelines

The manual is a self instructional workbook which contains operational procedures for changing old patterns of action into new ones. The reader can benefit by practicing the exercises contained and by reading and studying the manual as a reference textbook.

Awareness training, bodywork, martial arts, and spirit work are included in the manual as well as the advanced tactical ideas of the First Earth Battalion itself. Visual concepts will help the reader grasp many of the multi-dimensional ideas. A bibliography is included for further study. Where possible, names and addresses of various groups are included for the training described.

The ideas included are the most powerful and workable concepts gleaned from visits to over one hundred advanced human performance useful for many to do the work in some detail and then periodically use the pages as "flash cards" to keep their awareness at the highest useful level.

This manual is experimental and will be revised after the first limited edition goes out... is critiqued... added to... and refined for mass consumption. The drawings and verbiage were executed by Jim Channon after each of his visits. The follow-up manuals or supplements promise to continue these reports from the frontier of the third wave world.

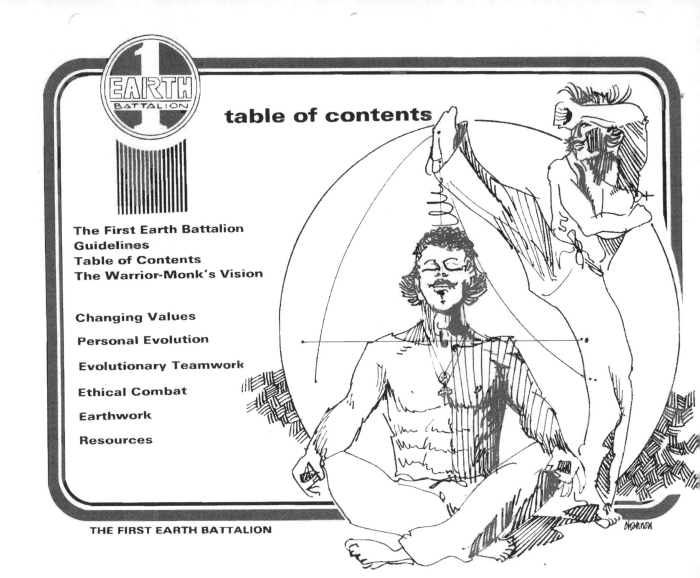

table of contents

THE FIRST EARTH BATTALION

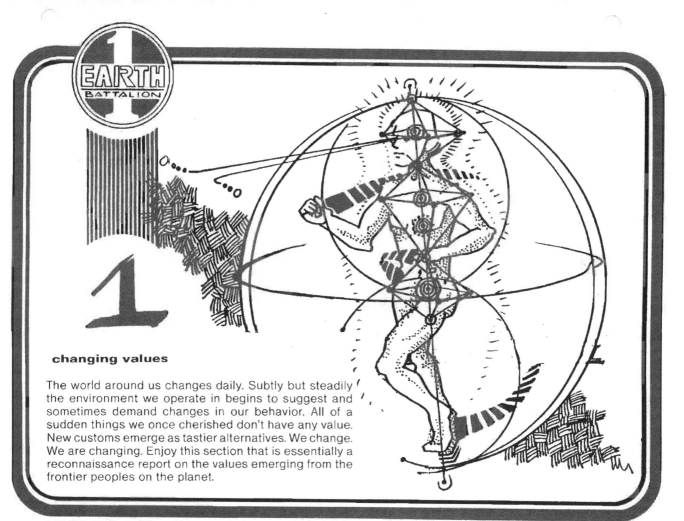

1

changing values

The world around us changes daily. Subtly but steadily the environment we operate in begins to suggest and sometimes demand changes in our behavior. All of a sudden things we once cherished don't have any value. New customs emerge as tastier alternatives. We change. We are changing. Enjoy this section that is essentially a reconnaissance report on the values emerging from the frontier peoples on the planet.

THE FIRST EARTH BATTALION

As our life experience changes we change what we value. American' has been changing what it values at an unprecedented rate since it became a nation.

One trend has become obvious. The coastal areas and large cities lead the value-changing phenomenon. It is often ten years before the values developed in Los Angeles find themselves into rural Arkansas.

Therefore, like it or not, what is developing today on the coasts will be the national value set roughly ten years from now. The reason this whole subject has relevance is because of the planning process used by large organizations. Evolutionaries must align their plans with the evolving values ten years out. What kind of Army will the American public expect in 1990? What kind of cities will be successful? What will be the state of marriage then? The evolutionary pays attention to the future value systems since they are the best guides to what will be *acceptable* and therefore workable.

The change process also requires lead time if it is to be evolutionary rather than revolutionary. So, focusing on the need ten years out allows time for planning, adjustment and the other growing pains associated with change to occur naturally. To plan for success we must know what people will value. Open your perspective with the study of the following evolving values:

THE FIRST EARTH BATTALION

those who strive after the truth and travel extensively in their quest are known as warriors. they are capable... they get the job done. good soldiers are also known as warriors. THE FIRST EARTH wants the action orientation of the warrior... but tempered with the patience and sensitivity and ethics of the monk. these are the soldiers who have the power to make paradise. Why go for anything less.

THE FIRST EARTH BATTALION

changing values

		OLD PARADIGM	NEW PARADIGM
POWER & POLITICS	1.	Impetus toward strong central government.	Favors reversing trend, decentralizing government wherever feasible; horizontal distribution of power.
	2.	Either pragmatic or visionary.	Pragmatic *and* visionary.
	3.	Government to keep people in line (disciplinary role) or as benevolent parent.	Government to foster growth, creativity, cooperation, transformation, synergy.
	4.	Humankind as conqueror of nature; exploitive view of resources.	Humankind in partnership with nature. Emphasis on conservation, ecological sanity.
ECONOMICS	1.	Promotes consumption at all costs, via planned obsolescence, advertising pressure, creation of artificial "needs".	Appropriate consumption. Conserving, keeping, recycling, quality, craftsmanship.
	2.	Aggression, competition. "Business is business".	Cooperation. Human values transcend "winning". As in New Games: "Play hard, play fair, nobody hurt".
	3.	Short-sighted: exploitation of limited resources.	Ecologically sensitive to ultimate costs. Stewardship.
	4.	"Rational", trusting only data.	Rational and intuitive. Data logic augmented by hunches, feelings, insights, nonlinear (holistic) sense of pattern.
	5.	Centralized operations.	Decentralized operations wherever possible. Human scale.
MEDICINE	1.	Treatment of symptoms.	Search for patterns and causes, plus treatment of symptoms.
	2.	Professional should be emotionally neutral.	Professional's caring is a component of healing.
	3.	Body and mind are separate; psychosomatic illness is mental, may be referred to psychiatrist.	Bodymind perspective; psychosomatic illness is province of all health-care professionals.
	4.	Placebo effect shows the power of suggestions.	Placebo effect shows the mind's role in disease and healing.
EDUCATION	1.	Emphasis on *content*, acquiring a body of "right" information, once and for all.	Emphasis on learning how to learn, how to ask good questions, pay attention to the right things, be open to and evaluate new concepts, have access to information. What is now "known" may change. Importance of *context*.
	2.	Learning as a *product*, a destination.	Learning as a *process*, a journey.
	3.	Priority on performance.	Priority on self-image as the generator of performance.
	4.	Emphasis on analytical, linear, left-brain thinking.	Strives for whole-brain education. Augments left-brain rationality with holistic, nonlinear, and intuitive strategies.
	5.	Concern with norms.	Concern with the individual's performance in terms of potential.

" A leaderless but powerful network is now working to bring about radical (but positive) change in the United States. Its members have broken with certain elements of Western thought, and may even have broken continuity with history "

...marilyn Ferguson
THE AQUARIAN CONSPIRACY   ST. MARTINS
                           PRESS N.Y.

THE FIRST EARTH BATTALION

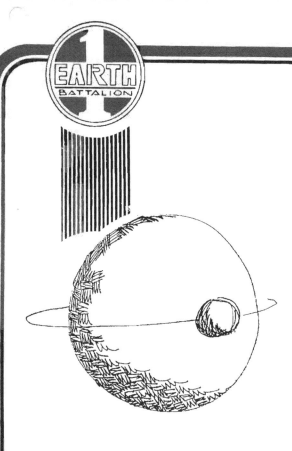

1 EARTH BATTALION

there is 5000 years of evidence that evolution is a constant. Higher states of order and co-operation continue to be the trend... for all systems.

Earthkind has grown from pack to village... and then from village to tribe... then from tribe to territory & from territory to nation.

It's time to go from nation to planet.

THE FIRST EARTH BATTALION declares its primary allegiance to the PLANET... "our home".

THE FIRST EARTH BATTALION

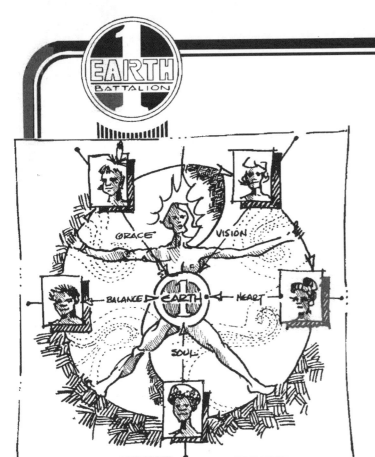

the possible human takes the power for service from the best qualities found in each race. the black race gives us our soul and the capacity to feel and taste the moment. the brown race gives us our heart and the capacity to hit the extremes with life and with each other. the white race gives us our vision and the capacity to imagine what is not and plan to get there. the red race gives us our grace and the capacity to live in harmony with mother EARTH. the yellow race gives us our balance and the capacity to integrate all the other dimensions without getting stuck in any one of them.

OBVIOUSLY .. EACH RACE HAS SOME OF ALL THE QUALITIES EXPRESSED .. WHAT HAS BEEN SELECTED ARE THOSE SPECIAL QUALITIES UNIQUELY NEEDED FOR THE LARGER BLEND FOR ALL HUMANKIND.

THE FIRST EARTH BATTALION

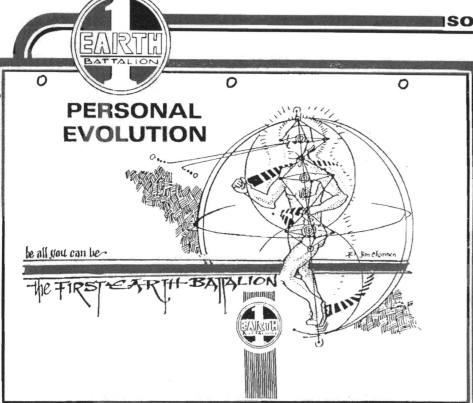

PERSONAL EVOLUTION

be all you can be

The FIRST EARTH BATTALION

there are many cultural pressures against improving yourself.

SELF·INDULGENCE

has been a label used to stiffle many of the human potential courses.

the fact is... you have very little you can contribute to others if you don't keep yourself in evolutionary shape!

we don't really have any serious alternative than to be _wonderful_!

THE FIRST EARTH BATTALION

Expanding ourselves
and our systems
into higher states
of order should be
the primary curriculum
for any discipline.

Put this material
in a binder and
begin to navigate
through the wonder.

EVOLUTIONARY TACTICS

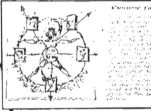

THE FIRST EARTH BATTALION

EARTH 1 BATTALION

All nations and all peoples have been represented in the roots of this country.

Warriors of the spirit can see many values captured in the most widely communicated piece of printed material in history... THE ONE DOLLAR BILL.

First, E PLURIBUS UNUM describes the mixing of the races... an ultimate mission.

Next, the eagle faces the olive branch indicating peace is the preferred tactic.

Finally, the pryamid is capped by the spiritual eye indicating the order of the ages is to be completed by... THE SPIRIT.

It is America's role to lead the world to paradise.

THE FIRST EARTH BATTALION

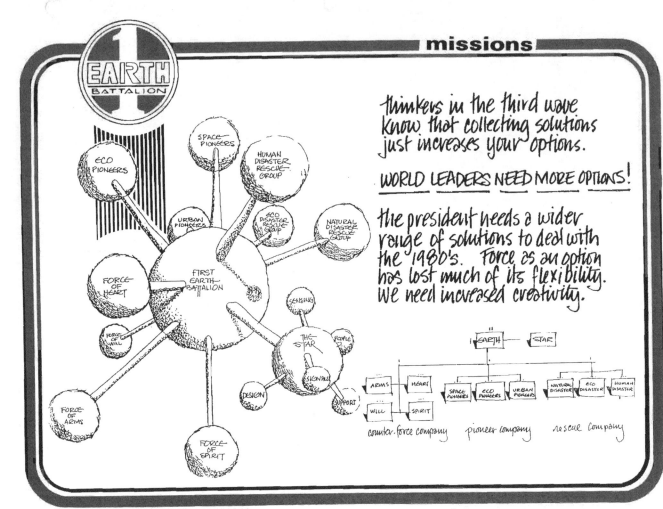

thinkers in the third wave
know that collecting solutions
just increases your options.

WORLD LEADERS NEED MORE OPTIONS!

the president needs a wider
range of solutions to deal with
the 1980's. Force as an option
has lost much of its flexibility.
we need increased creativity.

THE FIRST EARTH BATTALION

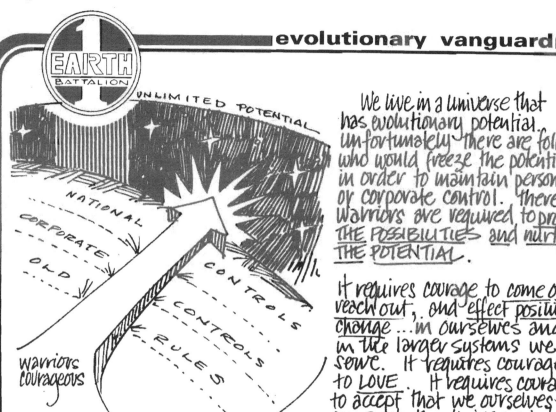

We live in a universe that has evolutionary potential. Unfortunately there are folks who would freeze the potential in order to maintain personal or corporate control. Therefore warriors are required to protect THE POSSIBILITIES and nurture THE POTENTIAL.

It requires courage to come out, reach out, and effect positive change... in ourselves and in the larger systems we serve. It requires courage to LOVE. It requires courage to accept that we ourselves can push the universe into higher states of order.

THE FIRST EARTH BATTALION

MACROBIOTICS

Bahä'i Faith

new Dimensions FOUNDATION

beyond jogging

In the flow

Berkeley Institute for Training in Psychodrama

DMA
DIMENSIONAL MIND APPROACH

the **Owner Builder Center**

The Center for Release and Integration

Postural Integration
Reichian Release
Rebirthing

BRIARPATCH REVIEW

A JOURNAL OF RIGHT LIVELIHOOD & SIMPLE LIVING

NEW AGE AWARENESS FAIR

A Center for Nutrition and Natural Healing

The **Biofeedback Center** of Berkeley

INTEGRAL CHUAN INSTITUTE

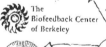

Aikido with Ki

YOU CAN LOSE WEIGHT

FAT LIBERATION

GENTLE WIND

the pioneering spirit is not dead in America! Many of the EARTH BN. ideas are taken from the NEW AGE. this small sample of new age groups shows there is plenty of gold left in the hills of the mind, body and spirit. the rush is on!

SPECTRUM SUITE: 7 selections of sound and color are programmed to resonate the 7 chakras. Steven Halpern, solo electric piano. Side II features flute.
STARBORN SUITE: "Music of the spheres." Steven Halpern, electric and acoustic keyboards. (Side II recorded 'live' at Findhorn.)

Our Ecotopia – a bold wholistic vision of future N.W. (Big Sur to B.C.) becoming a natural nation. Rooted in Bucky Fuller's *Synergetics*, Yoga & radical therapies, we give unique media shows.

halpern sounds

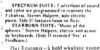

Arica.

Arica is a school for self-realization and the clarification of consciousness. We offer trainings, short programs and products for better health and balance of the body, emotions, mind and spirit. Arica offers a complete system and a proven method for understanding yourself, other people and the world around you.

The Brosnan Tortoise is a small group who seek to advance the comprehension, experience and worship of God.
Our activities center around the study of *The Urantia Book*. Anyone interested in this study is welcome to attend our regular reading and discussion sessions.

COMMUNITY RESEARCH AND EDUCATION

DAYSPRING, INC.

Isolation Tanks provide an ideal environment for: relaxation and stress reduction; meditation, the exploration of consciousness.
The Isolation Tank Program, offered by Dayspring, Inc., provides the opportunity for you to experience the tank environment in several ways.

THE FIRST EARTH BATTALION

EARTH
1
BATTALION

THIS TYPE OF LANGUAGE	PROMOTES THIS TYPE OF EFFECTIVENESS
VERBAL (WORDS)	LINEAR, DESCRIPTIVE, ANALYTICAL AND INCREMENTAL COGNITIVE WORK
GRAPHIC (MODELS)	DYNAMIC, INTERDEPENDENT, SYNTHETIC, AND HOLISTIC CONCEPTUAL WORK
CHRONOLOGIC (NET FLOW DIAGRAMS)	SEQUENTIAL, INTERDEPENDENT, TIME BASED, AND COMPLEX EVENTS OR CONSTRUCTION WORK
MATHEMATIC (NUMBERS)	ACCOUNTING, SUPPLY, MONEY AND OTHER DIGITAL RESOURCE WORK
KINESTHETIC (BODY CONTROL)	CONSERVATION, STRENGTH, ENERGY, CONTROL AND OTHER ANOLOGIC WORK
CORPORATE (MEETINGS / RITUALS)	SMALL GROUP RELATIONS, COOPERATIVE PLANNING AND OTHER WORK OF COMMITMENT TO PURPOSE
BONDING (DANCING / HUGGING / SINGING)	INDIVIDUAL OPENNESS AND THE DEVELOPMENT OF UNCONDITIONAL LOVE FOR OTHER HUMAN BEINGS.

PEOPLE WHO SCREAM THEY WANT MORE READING / WRITING / & ARITHMATIC DESERVE THE LIMITED WORLD THEY GET WITH THAT LIMITED SET OF LANGUAGES.

THE FIRST EARTH BATTALION

Words are just one of a number of powerful languages!

If you don't have a language to process a new set of possibilities then you will never know they are there. So, the widest range of understanding comes to those who have the widest range of language. Those who, likewise, have the greatest range of response to a given problem then have the greatest chance to respond adequately.

EARTH
BATTALION

colorful _and_ functional

we foster individuality ...and celebrate the way all ~humans are unique.

Costuming is becoming the prerogative of the individual.

A culture will emerge that has all the richness of a tribal culture with the function required of high tech.

The individual will shine through the uniformity

THE FIRST EARTH BATTALION

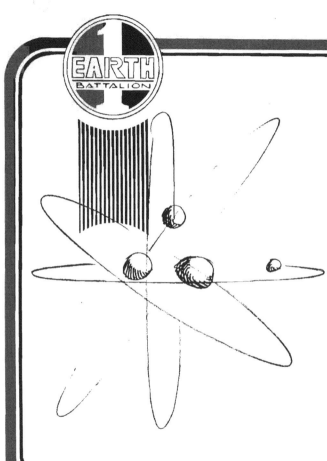

Everyone in the FIRST EARTH is equally important in the eyes of the organization and will be provided for accordingly.

Status is achieved by the skill and dedication with which you do your chosen tasks. It is not considered important that everyone move up in the organization ... only that their skill level moves up.

Leaders will be determined by those possessing group process skills and the other peculiar attributes of a leader.

THE FIRST EARTH BATTALION

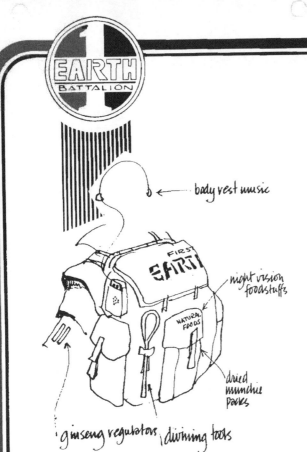

body vest music

night vision foodstuffs

NATURAL FOODS

dried munchie packs

ginseng regulators   divining tools

technology and human potential don't have to be adversary positions.. we can use advanced machinery and advanced people.

likewise the idealists on the right and the idealists on the left would do better for all if they worked on the same team.

get comfortable with combining positions and not choosing sides.

this is the third wave way.

THE FIRST EARTH BATTALION

STATES OF SUCCESSIVE EXPANSION

the challenge is to become a "wide-band operator... and make more frequent trips to each new state. most folks stop at low order reasoning. the worst become MICRONAUTS OR STAGNANTS.

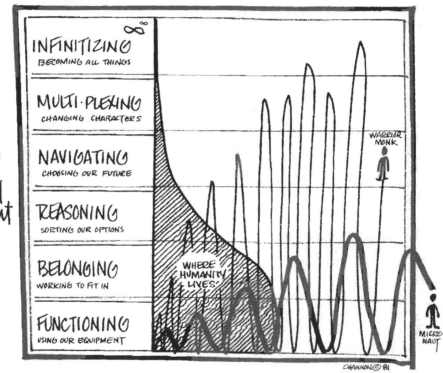

INFINITIZING	BECOMING ALL THINGS
MULTI-PLEXING	CHANGING CHARACTERS
NAVIGATING	CHOOSING OUR FUTURE
REASONING	SORTING OUR OPTIONS
BELONGING	WORKING TO FIT IN
FUNCTIONING	USING OUR EQUIPMENT

WHERE HUMANITY LIVES

WARRIOR MONK

MICRO-NAUT

CHANNON © 81

THE FIRST EARTH BATTALION

a new class of humans is emerging..who refuse to sink into the ever pervasive CULTURAL TRANCE. A cultural trance is a collection of perceptions that cause the sleeping human to believe they have no power to change themselves or the world around them.

THE FIRST EARTH BATTALION

1 EARTH BATTALION

THE WARRIOR MONK
GUILTY OF BEING IN SERVICE TO THE PLANET.... USUALLY AT THE RISK OF BEING LABELLED A "FLAKE". IS CHARGED WITH CONTINUOUSLY WORKING ON UNREALISTIC CONCEPTS LIKE WORLD PEACE AND BROTHERLY LOVE. REALLY BELIEVES SOLDIERS CAN PLAY A LEAD ROLE IN WORLD PEACE.

THE CAREERIST
GUILTY OF BEING IN SERVICE TO HIMSELF.... USUALLY AT HIS PEERS EXPENSE. CHARGED WITH CONSISTENT WEASEL-WORDING AND FRAUDULENT BEAN COUNTING TO COVER INCOMPETENCE & THE FACTS, IN ORDER TO GET PROMOTED. REALLY BELIEVES YOU GOTTA TAKE CARE OF NUMBER ONE FIRST.

THE MILITARIST
GUILTY OF BEING IN SERVICE TO THE SERVICE .... USUALLY AT THE TAX-PAYERS EXPENSE. CHARGED WITH UNCONSCIOUSLY PUSHING MILITARY PROGRAMS AND WEAPONS CONTRACTS THAT EXCEED DEFENSE NEEDS. REALLY BELIEVES THE NATION SHOULD BE CALLED UP TO DEFEND THE ARMY.

THE PROFESSIONAL SOLDIER.
GUILTY OF BEING IN SERVICE TO THE NATION AND HIS TROOPS ...USUALLY AT SOME RISK TO HIS CAREER. IS CHARGED WITH TELLING THE TRUTH EVEN WHEN IT HURTS AND GIVING THE TAXPAYER HIS MONEY'S WORTH. REALLY BELIEVES IN TAKING CARE OF SOLDIERS AND MISSION FIRST.

can you trace the values shift in the military?

THE FIRST EARTH BATTALION

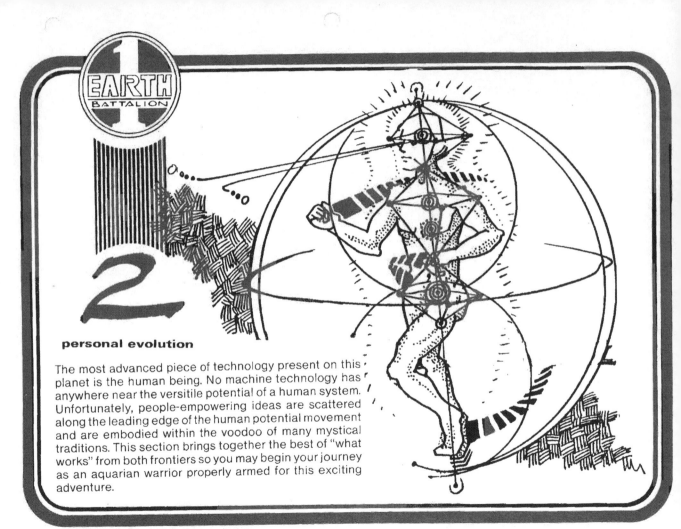

1 EARTH BATTALION

2

personal evolution

The most advanced piece of technology present on this planet is the human being. No machine technology has anywhere near the versitile potential of a human system. Unfortunately, people-empowering ideas are scattered along the leading edge of the human potential movement and are embodied within the voodoo of many mystical traditions. This section brings together the best of "what works" from both frontiers so you may begin your journey as an aquarian warrior properly armed for this exciting adventure.

THE FIRST EARTH BATTALION

personal evolution

The universe is perfect just as it is. It gives you, the individual, just what you need and no more. In this way you can experience a progressively more interesting life from moment to moment. When you cooperate with the universe, it makes this trip into an expanded awareness; a smooth and delicious experience. When you ignore the evolutionary masterplan, the universe will expand your awareness just the same, but the trip is then bumpy and often very painful. In this section of the manual you will be given insight into some time honored and also some new technology needed to make your personal adventure in this world both creative and enjoyable.

The manual focuses on key evolutionary actions that you can master. These actions can create positive visions for you that will change your life the very moment you begin practicing them. These actions will enable you to steer your awareness and therfore evaluate your experience through what have been heretofore boring or painful moments.

There are many ways to experience each moment. Some people seem to enjoy them all. Some masters can experience many of them in various states of ecstacy. But we know for most people, life has its ups and downs, and then there are some people who manage not to enjoy any of it at all.

Gaining leverage over the life experience can come through a key set of lessons for both success and enlightenment. Fortunately, the best schools on the subject moved to the United States in recent years and were available for our research. The following key technology has been selected from the works of over a hundred schools both orthodox and mystical, traditional and futuristic, and specially oriented on the paths of both personal and planetary evolution. These tools will work for you to the extent that you use them. That's a promise.

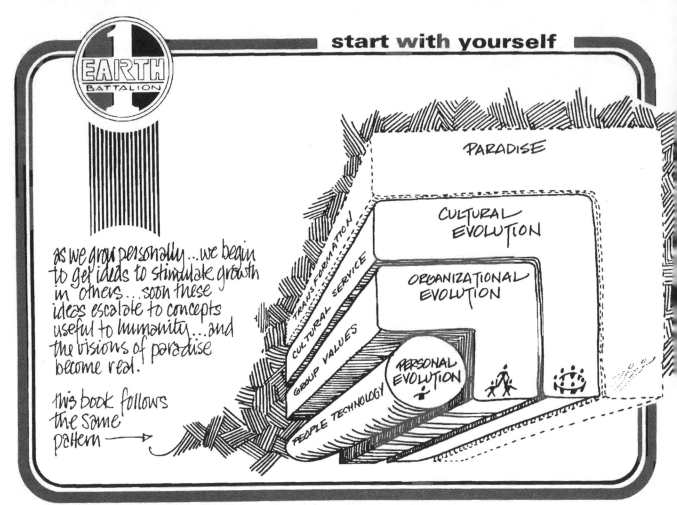

as we grow personally...we begin to get ideas to stimulate growth in others...soon these ideas escalate to concepts useful to humanity...and the visions of paradise become real.

this book follows the same pattern →

PARADISE

CULTURAL EVOLUTION

ORGANIZATIONAL EVOLUTION

PERSONAL EVOLUTION

TRANSFORMATION

CULTURAL SERVICE

GROUP VALUES

PEOPLE TECHNOLOGY

THE FIRST EARTH BATTALION

1

EARTH

BATTALI

What are the limits to human potential? In the final analysis they seem to be a bad joke. The culture imposes a language of the possible. Most humans accept those limits and fail to increase their potential. But where those limits are ignored.. people bend metal with their minds, walk on fire, calculate faster than a computer, travel to new places in their minds eye, stop their hearts with no ill effects and see into the future. There are no limits in the EARTH BATTALION.

THE FIRST EARTH BATTALION

the path of personal evolution

the path to enlightened living... is also the path to effective action.

fill from the bottom ...when you hit love you're on a rocket ship for the rest of the trip...

FREEDOM

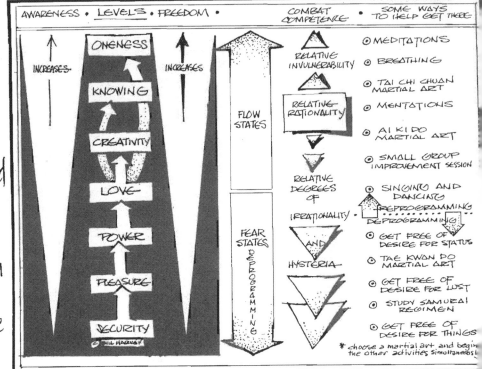

AWARENESS • LEVELS • FREEDOM •	COMBAT COMPETENCE	SOME WAYS TO HELP GET THERE

INCREASES — ONENESS — INCREASES

KNOWING

CREATIVITY

LOVE

POWER

PLEASURE

SECURITY

FLOW STATES — RELATIVE INVULNERABILITY

RELATIVE RATIONALITY

RELATIVE DEGREES OF IRRATIONALITY

FEAR STATES — DEPROGRAMMING — AND HYSTERIA

⊙ MEDITATIONS
⊙ BREATHING
⊙ TAI CHI CHUAN MARTIAL ART
⊙ MENTATIONS
⊙ AI KI DO MARTIAL ART
⊙ SMALL GROUP IMPROVEMENT SESSION
⊙ SINGING AND DANCING REPROGRAMMING
DEPROGRAMMING
⊙ GET FREE OF DESIRE FOR STATUS
⊙ TAE KWON DO MARTIAL ART
⊙ GET FREE OF DESIRE FOR LUST
⊙ STUDY SAMURAI REGIMEN
⊙ GET FREE OF DESIRE FOR THINGS

* choose a martial art and begin the other activities simultaneously

THE FIRST EARTH BATTALION

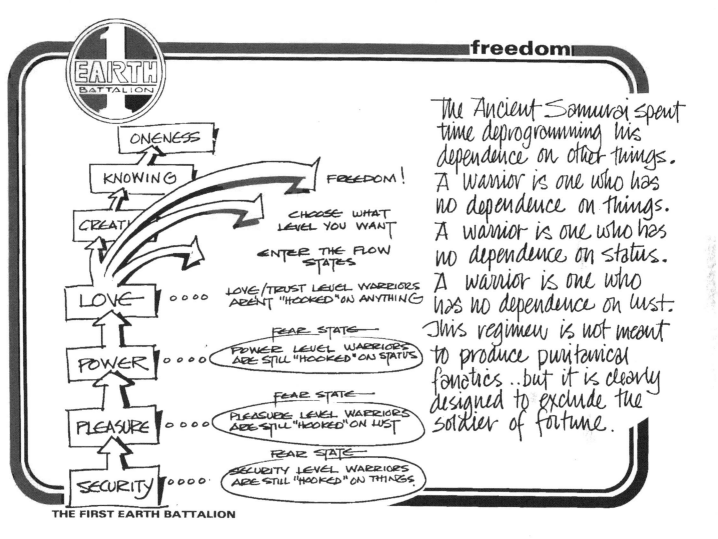

EARTH BATTALION 1

ONENESS

KNOWING

FREEDOM!

CREATI

CHOOSE WHAT
LEVEL YOU WANT

ENTER THE FLOW
STATES

LOVE — o o o o — LOVE/TRUST LEVEL WARRIORS
AREN'T "HOOKED" ON ANYTHING

FEAR STATE
POWER — o o o o — POWER LEVEL WARRIORS
ARE STILL "HOOKED" ON STATUS

FEAR STATE
PLEASURE — o o o o — PLEASURE LEVEL WARRIORS
ARE STILL "HOOKED" ON LUST

FEAR STATE
SECURITY — o o o o — SECURITY LEVEL WARRIORS
ARE STILL "HOOKED" ON THINGS.

THE FIRST EARTH BATTALION

The Ancient Samurai spent time deprogramming his dependence on other things. A warrior is one who has no dependence on things. A warrior is one who has no dependence on status. A warrior is one who has no dependence on lust. This regimen is not meant to produce puritanical fanatics .. but it is clearly designed to exclude the soldier of fortune.

1
EARTH
BATTALION

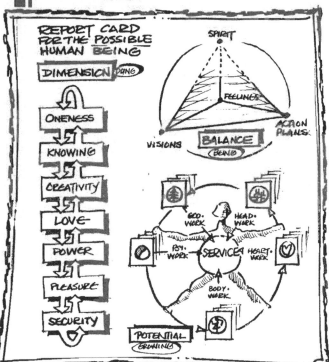

REPORT CARD
FOR THE POSSIBLE
HUMAN BEING

DIMENSION (DOING)

↓
ONENESS
⇅
KNOWING
⇅
CREATIVITY
⇅
LOVE
⇅
POWER
⇅
PLEASURE
⇅
SECURITY
↓

SPIRIT
FEELINGS
ACTION PLANS
VISIONS
BALANCE (BEING)

GOD. WORK   HEAD. WORK
PSY. WORK   SERVICE   HEART. WORK
BODY. WORK

POTENTIAL (GROWING)

THE FIRST EARTH BATTALION

We are many things now...we can be many more.... simultaneously. We can have great Dimension by daily cruising the scale of needs. At one end taking care of business and at the other taking care of spirit. ...We can simultaneously balance our mental approach during each event.... touching feelings.. having visions and verbalizing solutions.... while staying in touch with the overall quality of our spirit. We can plan our growth omni directionally guided by the strengths of the races. check yourself now... how's your BEING, DOING, AND GROWING.

EARTH 1 BATTALION

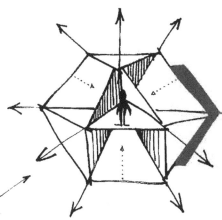

Bucky Fuller's vector equilibrium illustrates how you can open up in many directions simultaneously and thereby secure the best combination of dynamic tension and integrity... GROW OUT.

By generating an environment of loving support, we can encourage people to OPEN UP.

Within that structure the individual is safe and trusting... at that moment the powers & skills that are within us all can come rushing out.. effortlessly and joyously.

Whats so amazing is that the structure is not material at all it is LOVE.

THE FIRST EARTH BATTALION

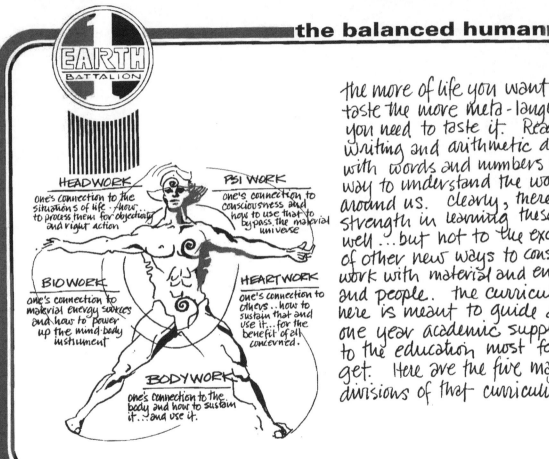

EARTH 1 BATTALION

HEADWORK
one's connection to the situations of life. How to process them for objectivity and right action

PSI WORK
one's connection to consciousness and how to use that to bypass the material universe

BIO WORK
one's connection to material energy sources and how to power up the mind-body instrument

HEARTWORK
one's connection to others.. how to sustain that and use it... for the benefit of all concerned.

BODYWORK
one's connection to the body and how to sustain it... and use it.

the more of life you want to taste the more meta-languages you need to taste it. Reading, writing and arithmetic deal with words and numbers as a way to understand the world around us. clearly, there is strength in learning these tools well ... but not to the exclusion of other new ways to constructively work with material and energy and people. the curriculum here is meant to guide a one year academic supplement to the education most folks get. Here are the five majors divisions of that curriculum.

THE FIRST EARTH BATTALION

EARTH **1** BATTALION

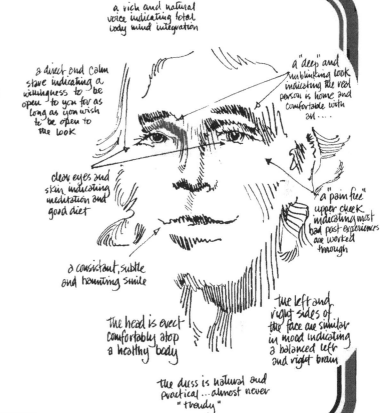

How do people look when they are "whole"... together... in charge of themselves and in charge of their bodies? How do people look when they have coughed up all the pain buried deep in their psyche and deep in their muscle structure? How do people look when they are centered... grounded... and focused? How do people look when they <u>know</u> for a fact that the universe (GOD) has a positive plan for mankind? How do people look when they <u>know</u> they have an active role in that plan? Here are some clues!

a rich and natural voice indicating total body mind integration

a direct and calm stare indicating a willingness to be open to you for as long as you wish to be open to the look

a "deep" and unblinking look indicating the real person is home and comfortable with an....

clear eyes and skin indicating meditation and good diet

a "pain free" upper cheek indicating most bad past experiences are worked through

a consistant, subtle and haunting smile

the head is erect comfortably atop a healthy body

the left and right sides of the face are similar in mood indicating a balanced left and right brain

the dress is natural and practical... almost never "trendy"

THE FIRST EARTH BATTALION

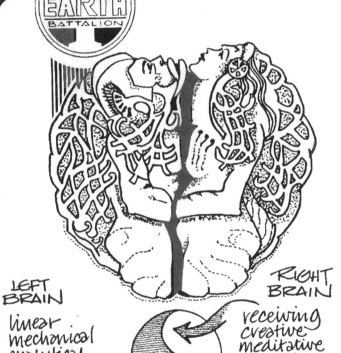

1 EARTH BATTALION

LEFT BRAIN

linear
mechanical
analytical
logical
routine memory
verbal

RIGHT BRAIN

receiving
creative
meditative
artistic
intuitive
spatial

There really doesn't seem to be any excuse for today's warrior to be anything less than androgynous. If the warrior intends to follow the time honored indirect approach recommended by master strategist B.H. Liddell Hart, then the development of the right brain is in order. The best traits of both sexes will develop the balance required for the work of peacemakers.

EARTH 1 BATTALION

Does your costume communicate? If not you're missing a FREEBEE. the tribe is coming back.

The American Indian revealed himself as an individual by his distinctive ornamentation. His shield in some cases was more complete as a representation of his skills and predispositions than the modern soldiers personnel file.

EARTH BATTALION soldiers will be encouraged to represent them-selves well in their dress, and wear a 12 pointed star with each axis clipped to reveal a dimension on a standard personality inventory test.

THE FIRST EARTH BATTALION

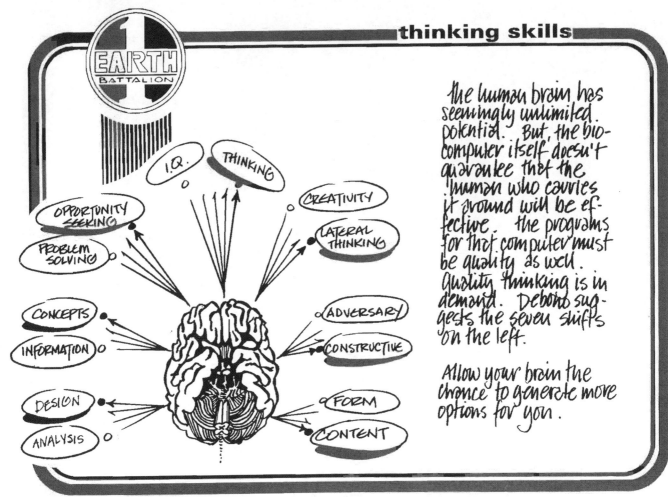

1 EARTH BATTALION

I.Q.

THINKING

CREATIVITY

LATERAL THINKING

OPPORTUNITY SEEKING

PROBLEM SOLVING

CONCEPTS

INFORMATION

ADVERSARY

CONSTRUCTIVE

DESIGN

ANALYSIS

FORM

CONTENT

the human brain has seemingly unlimited potential. But, the bio-computer itself doesn't guarantee that the human who carries it around will be ef-fective. the programs for that computer must be quality as well. Quality thinking is in demand. Debono sug-gests the seven shifts on the left.

Allow your brain the chance to generate more options for you.

THE FIRST EARTH BATTALION

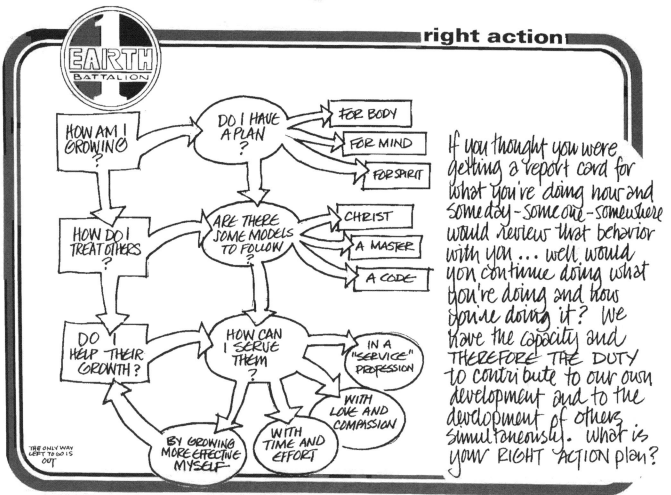

EARTH BATTALION 1

HOW AM I GROWING?

DO I HAVE A PLAN?
→ FOR BODY
→ FOR MIND
→ FOR SPIRIT

HOW DO I TREAT OTHERS?

ARE THERE SOME MODELS TO FOLLOW?
→ CHRIST
→ A MASTER
→ A CODE

DO I HELP THEIR GROWTH?

HOW CAN I SERVE THEM?
→ IN A "SERVICE" PROFESSION
→ WITH LOVE AND COMPASSION
→ WITH TIME AND EFFORT
→ BY GROWING MORE EFFECTIVE MYSELF

THE ONLY WAY LEFT TO GO IS OUT

If you thought you were getting a report card for what you're doing now and someday-someone-somewhere would review that behavior with you ... well would you continue doing what you're doing and how you're doing it? We have the capacity and THEREFORE THE DUTY to contribute to our own development and to the development of others simultaneously. What is your RIGHT ACTION plan?

THE FIRST EARTH BATTALION

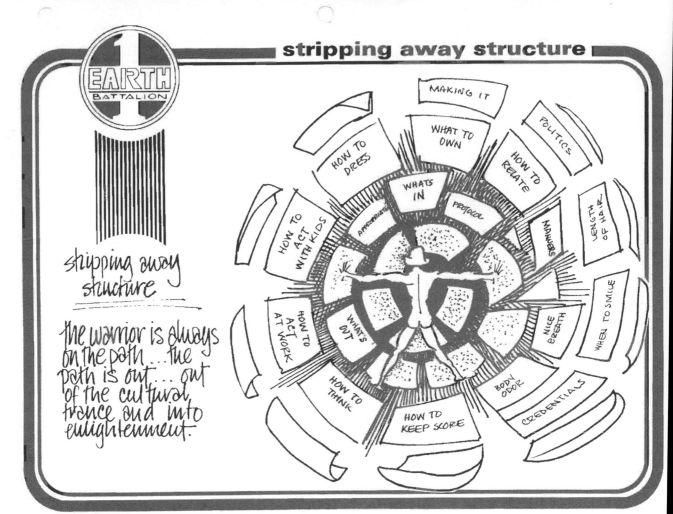

stripping away
structure

the warrior is always
on the path... the
path is out... out
of the cultural
trance and into
enlightenment.

THE FIRST EARTH BATTALION

work areas

objective measures of performance

area	level 1	level 2	level 3	level 4	level 5	level 6
BODYWORK	can take a fall	can take a blow	can do 10 Km under an hour	has a belt in a martial art	has a black belt in a martial art	has two black belts
BIOWORK	can fast on juice a week	does nuts & grains one month	massages & cleanses colon	can process pranayama	is 90%-plus a vegetarian	can live off nature twenty days
HEADWORK	recognizes own cultural programs	stops using mindless cliches	identifies feelings separately	eliminates habits of all kinds	can visually model what's happening	can previsualise a more useful alternative
HEARTWORK	knows heart can control the action	understands heart language	opens the heart chakra	can mirror heart & breath of another	can fall in love with everyone	can perform a heart ceremony
SPIRITWORK	can feel spirit	connects the spirit & man	realizes the different paths of spirit	can channel	operates based on spirit communications	can explain GOD as an engineer
PSIWORK	learns to release	hears & sees other's thoughts	can do out-of-body travel	can do some psychokinesis	can pass through objects	slips the silver lining
ECOWORK	stays out alone at night	can trace an ecosystem	maintains & eats veggies	can sense plant auras	organizes a tree-plant with kids	establishes an eco-project that someone else runs
PEACEWORK	has worked in the mainstream	understands the value of friction	understands distrust and hate	develops peace inside	develops peace in a team	becomes walking-talking peacemaker
FRAMEWORK	sees workplace from above	understands meta-view & metaphor	models an operating system	applies evolutionary management	applies techniques to larger system	actually changes a violent pattern in world

develop yourself a step at a time.

IT IS HERE YOU CAN BE CALLED A MASTER WARRIOR-MONK

THE FIRST EARTH BATTALION

these are the major areas of work for the warrior:

work	objective	reason	color
Bodywork	For physical control/power	To eliminate fear	Dark green
Bodywork	For stamina and control	To shun poison	Light green
Headwork	For flexible behavior	To be free of structure	Yellow
Heartwork	For connections to people	To be free of inferiority	Red
Spiritwork	For connections to spirit	To be free of loneliness	Purple
Psiwork	For connections to universe	To be free of your body	Violet
Ecowork	For connections to the biosphere	To be free of separation	Light blue
Peacework	For connections between people	To be free of tyranny	Dark blue
Framework	For restructuring organizations	To be free of stagnation	Orange

THE FIRST EARTH BATTALION

realization

BODYWORK

The moments when serenity guides your physical conflicts with another or your movement through life.

BIOWORK

The moment when the care of your body instrument is more important than the taste of the food in front of you.

HEADWORK

The moment you begin to see when you are just reacting from a mind program within a culturally induced trance.

HEARTWORK

The moment when you recognize that deep inside we are all one.

SPIRITWORK

The moment that you appreciate the perfect order in the universe, the biosphere and your mind. Then you will sense the power of a masterplan.

PSI WORK

The moment you feel the universe send its own kind of energy tingling through your body and your mind takes off.

ECOWORK

The moment that you know that the plants around you are conscious as well as the air and earth mother below.

PEACEWORK

The moment you dedicate your life to actions on behalf of PEOPLE AND PLANET ... *then* you have become a player.

FRAMEWORK

The moment you see you can step out of an organizational pattern and reprogram the system.

How will you know when you get there?

answer these states of being honestly.

and you will be there ...

THE FIRST EARTH BATTALION

this is a possible sequence
of actions for any team.

Its just not important that
we all do the same things.
Every team will be unique.
Once you get together you
will understand this
even better. Enjoy this adventure!

THE FIRST EARTH BATTALION

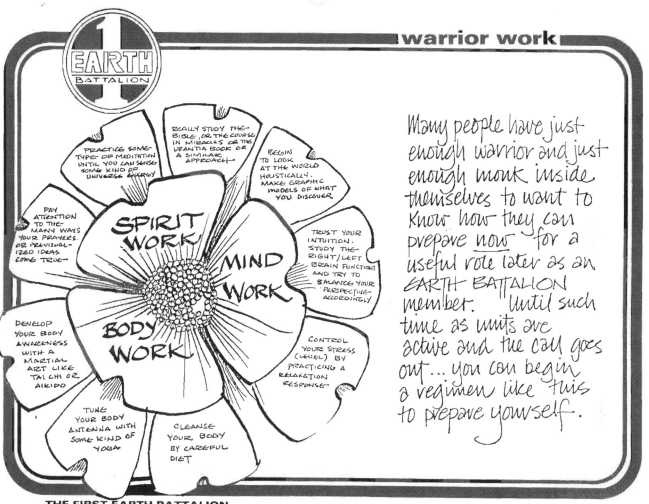

EARTH 1 BATTALION

SPIRIT WORK

PRACTICE SOME TYPE OF MEDITATION UNTIL YOU CAN SENSE SOME KIND OF UNIVERSE ENERGY

REALLY STUDY THE BIBLE, OR THE COURSE IN MIRACLES OR THE URANTIA BOOK OR A SIMILAR APPROACH

BEGIN TO LOOK AT THE WORLD HOLISTICALLY. MAKE GRAPHIC MODELS OF WHAT YOU DISCOVER

PAY ATTENTION TO THE MANY WAYS YOUR PRAYERS, OR PREVIZUAL-IZED IDEAS COME TRUE

MIND WORK

TRUST YOUR INTUITION. STUDY THE RIGHT/LEFT BRAIN FUNCTION AND TRY TO BALANCE YOUR PERSPECTIVE ACCORDINGLY

BODY WORK

DEVELOP YOUR BODY AWARENESS WITH A MARTIAL ART LIKE TAI CHI OR AIKIDO

CONTROL YOUR STRESS (LEVEL) BY PRACTICING A RELAXATION RESPONSE

TUNE YOUR BODY ANTENNA WITH SOME KIND OF YOGA

CLEANSE YOUR BODY BY CAREFUL DIET

THE FIRST EARTH BATTALION

Many people have just enough warrior and just enough monk inside themselves to want to know how they can prepare now for a useful role later as an EARTH BATTALION member. Until such time as units are active and the call goes out... you can begin a regimen like this to prepare yourself.

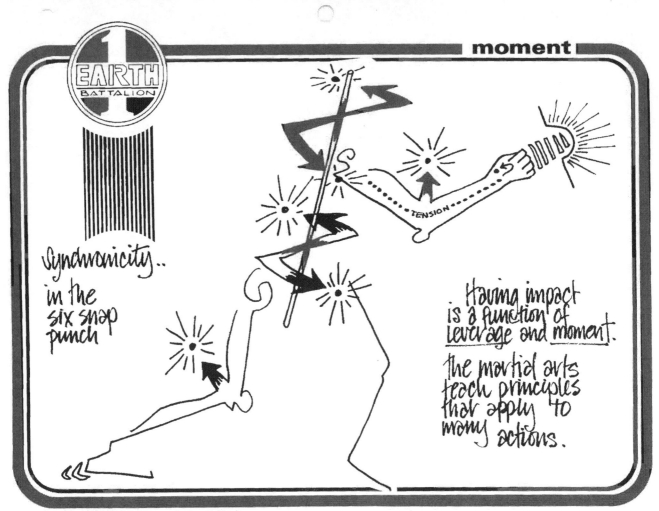

EARTH 1 BATTALION

synchronicity..
in the
six snap
punch

TENSION

. Having impact
is a function of
leverage and moment.

the martial arts
teach principles
that apply to
many actions.

THE FIRST EARTH BATTALION

Whether you are a single warrior or part of a unit, these principles apply:

The ethic here is one of "loving protection". These principles are a blend of those martial arts disciplines that have already struggled with the concepts of ethics.

They can apply to strategy as well as tactics.

CENTERING
CLEANING YOURSELF..FOCUSING INNER ENERGY...TAPPING INTO THE FORCE..THE COLLECTIVE EVOLUTIONARY PROCESS OF HUMANITY

GROUNDING
FEELING A CONNECTION WITH THE GROUND AND THE HEAVEN. MAKING THOSE AREAS CONTRI-BUTE TO YOUR ROOTS AND YOUR FLEXIBILITY.

SENSING
OPENING UP..EMPTYING OUT.. INCREASING YOUR OVERALL AWARENESS..NEVER BLOCK YOUR SENSING INSTRUMENTS.

BLENDING
SENSE THE OPPOSING ENERGY.. BLEND WITH IT OR REFLECT IT. LOOK FOR WEAKSPOTS IN ITS DECISION STRUCTURE OR POWER BASE.

LEVERAGING
TAKE JUST ENOUGH ENERGY AND APPLY IT AT KEY POINTS TO LEVERAGE THE OPPOSING FORCE GENTLY UNTIL IT SUBMITS TO YOUR CONTROL.

TEMPERING
SHOW THE OPPOSITION YOUR HEART AND AGREE TO DISENGAGE

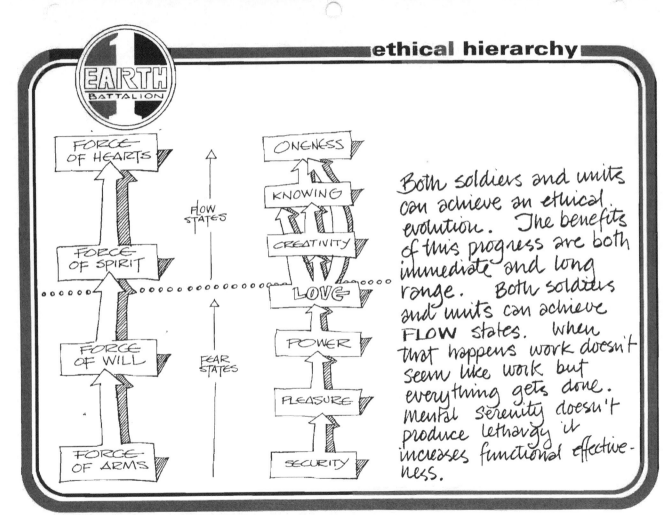

1 EARTH BATTALION

FORCE OF HEARTS

FORCE OF SPIRIT

FORCE OF WILL

FORCE OF ARMS

FLOW STATES

FEAR STATES

ONENESS

KNOWING

CREATIVITY

LOVE

POWER

PLEASURE

SECURITY

Both soldiers and units can achieve an ethical evolution. The benefits of this progress are both immediate and long range. Both soldiers and units can achieve FLOW states. When that happens work doesn't seem like work but everything gets done. Mental serenity doesn't produce lethargy it increases functional effectiveness.

THE FIRST EARTH BATTALION

EARTH BATTALION 1

Recent studies have shown clearly that we can effectively "PRACTICE" events in our minds. So, if there is something you would like to accomplish... do it in your mind first. Athletes have increased their performance dramatically with this picturing technique. when you think about it..this is the clearest way to send plans and orders to your body and psyche before you do something. PICTURE YOURSELF HEALTHY AND ENERGETIC..see if it catches!

I SEE MYSELF SPRING OUT OF BED......

I SEE MYSELF WALKING ENERGETICALLY AND CONFIDENTLY INTO WORK....

I LOOK INDEPENDENT, ERECT, FIT AND ABLE TO MAKE ANYTHING POSSIBLE...

I COMMUNICATE COMPASSIONATELY WITH SOMEONE WHO IS NOT IN CONTROL...

I TAKE A DIFFICULT BUT REAL PROBLEM AND SOLVE IT BY AN INDIRECT APPROACH....

I SEE PEOPLE WHO ARE GLAD TO HAVE ME AROUND...

I TELL THEM HOW GLAD I AM TO BE AROUND...

NATURALLY, THINGS GO WELL...I PLANNED IT THAT WAY.

PREVIEW A SUCCESSFUL TOMORROW

TV SCREEN

TO HELP YOU BEGIN, VISUALIZE A TV SCREEN IN YOUR HEAD

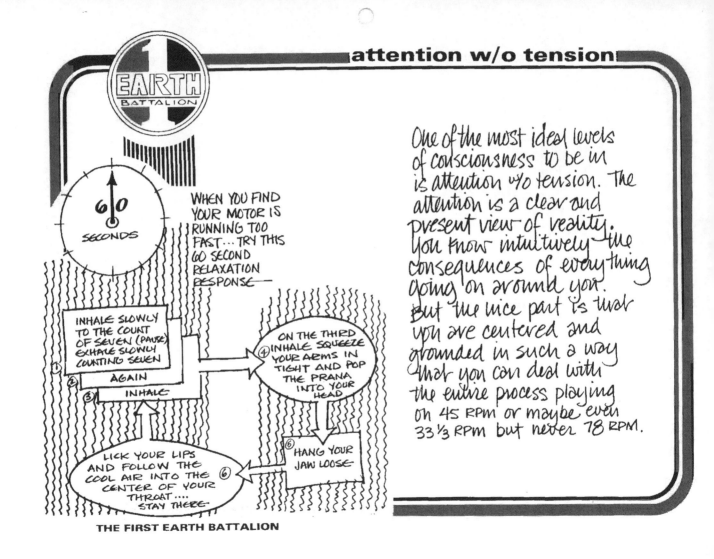

1 EARTH BATTALION

60 SECONDS

WHEN YOU FIND YOUR MOTOR IS RUNNING TOO FAST... TRY THIS 60 SECOND RELAXATION RESPONSE—

① INHALE SLOWLY TO THE COUNT OF SEVEN (PAUSE) EXHALE SLOWLY COUNTING SEVEN

② AGAIN

③ INHALE

④ ON THE THIRD INHALE SQUEEZE YOUR ARMS IN TIGHT AND POP THE PRANA INTO YOUR HEAD

⑤ HANG YOUR JAW LOOSE

⑥ LICK YOUR LIPS AND FOLLOW THE COOL AIR INTO THE CENTER OF YOUR THROAT.... STAY THERE-

THE FIRST EARTH BATTALION

One of the most ideal levels of consciousness to be in is attention w/o tension. The attention is a clear and present view of reality. You know intuitively the consequences of everything going on around you. But the nice part is that you are centered and grounded in such a way that you can deal with the entire process playing on 45 RPM or maybe even 33⅓ RPM but never 78 RPM.

EARTH BATTALION 1

It's not healthy and its not fun to hold on to ways of thinking that get in the way of our growth. it's astonishing how easy it is to give yourself permission to dump programs that don't work. "Cultural cripples" can be healed as fast as they want to be.

THE FIRST EARTH BATTALION

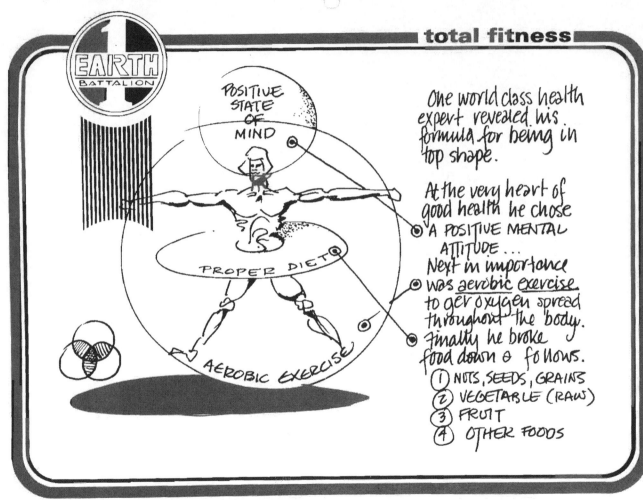

POSITIVE STATE OF MIND

PROPER DIET

AEROBIC EXERCISE

One world class health expert revealed his formula for being in top shape.

At the very heart of good health he chose A POSITIVE MENTAL ATTITUDE ...
Next in importance was <u>aerobic exercise</u>. to get oxygen spread throughout the body.
Finally he broke food down & follows.

1. NUTS, SEEDS, GRAINS
2. VEGETABLE (RAW)
3. FRUIT
4. OTHER FOODS

THE FIRST EARTH BATTALION

the meta.perspective... our view from the top. Become calm in what ever situation you find yourself. take a moment and step out of the situation. Essentially view the situation from above. Notice whats really going on.

Now you're in a much better position to decide how to have a positive influence on the personalities present. Never completely return to the event or you may become a reaction to it rather than a director of it.

THE FIRST EARTH BATTALION

Some people live <u>moment</u> <u>to</u> <u>moment</u>...they're outside. They can see the world from the outside...they <u>read</u> the music of life from the sheet with the notes printed on it. Other people live <u>in</u> <u>the</u> <u>moment</u> ...they're inside. They <u>feel</u> the world with their bodies and they <u>live</u> the music of life by grooving on the things and moods that come to them. The conscious warrior stays awake enough to <u>choose</u> the way to process experience to best support the mission of service <u>and</u> <u>enjoy</u> <u>it</u> !!

GO OUTSIDE ──➤

When working with others or doing "head work" it's good to go outside and check on your objectivity. How do you look...is it working?

3" BELOW NAVEL

GO INSIDE!
a warrior-monk who must go from point A to point B will shift his consciousness to his one point and REALLY GET INTO WALKING.

THE FIRST EARTH BATTALION

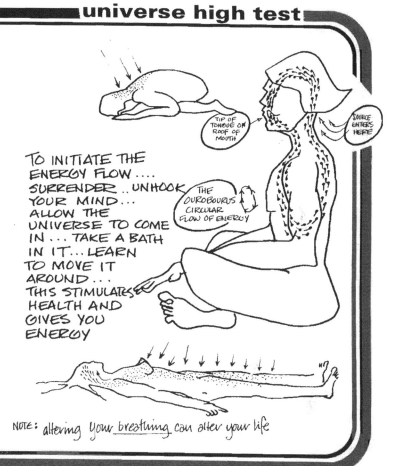

god and the magnificent universe soup we live in can kiss us with its basic free energy source. Some have called it prana. others just say they feel enveloped in a white light... others just say they experienced a rush of energy. the universe has ways to "enLIGHTen" us. it has ways to let us know when we're doing good work. good work makes you _feel_ GOOD. REAL GOOD!!

TO INITIATE THE ENERGY FLOW.... SURRENDER ..UNHOOK YOUR MIND... ALLOW THE UNIVERSE TO COME IN ... TAKE A BATH IN IT...LEARN TO MOVE IT AROUND ... THIS STIMULATES HEALTH AND GIVES YOU ENERGY

NOTE: altering your _breathing_ can alter your life

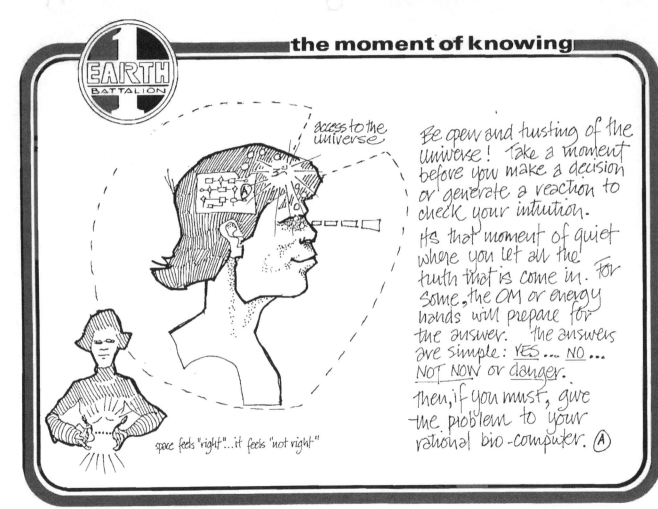

EARTH BATTALION 1

access to the universe

space feels "right"...it feels "not right"

Be open and trusting of the universe! Take a moment before you make a decision or generate a reaction to check your intuition.

It's that moment of quiet where you let all the truth that is come in. For some, the OM or energy hands will prepare for the answer. The answers are simple: <u>YES</u>... <u>NO</u>... <u>NOT NOW</u> or <u>danger</u>.

Then, if you must, give the problem to your rational bio-computer. (A)

THE FIRST EARTH BATTALION

EARTH 1 BATTALION

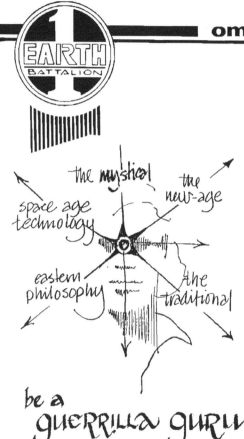

the mystical

space age technology

the new-age

eastern philosophy

the traditional

be a
GUERRILLA GURU

Collect strategies by collecting people and points of view. The more you own, the greater your chance of success in any situation.

OMNI-DIRECTIONAL THOUGHT

the first EARTH is not mission oriented it is potential oriented. That means we shall continue to look everywhere to find non-destructive methods of control.

J.F.C. Fuller, the father of mechanized warfare, was an omni-directional thinker and a member of the world of the mystical.

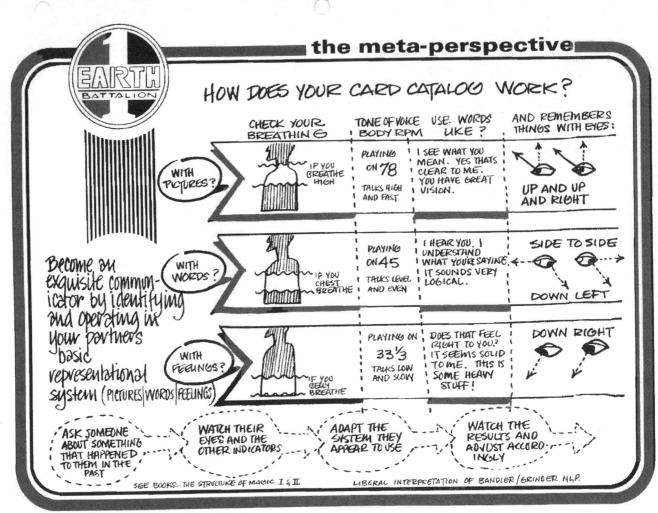

THE FIRST EARTH BATTALION

YOUTH IS AN UNDERRATED RESOURCE CAPABLE OF REFORESTING THE COUNTRY.

THE OLDER GENERATIONS COULD GREEN UP THE CITIES THEY BUILT.

UNDER WORKED

OVER WORKED

UNDER WORKED

there are no "old" people ....
there are just those who are
suffering from <u>hardening</u>
<u>of the concepts</u> ... the world
constantly gets more rich &
more aware ... new ideas and
a greater array of sensitivities.
embrace each new generation.
WE ARE GETTING BETTER.
Some cronologically old
people are as "new" as the
latest thing they learned.
they will play an important
role in the near future.
keep them in your net.
we are all one age if we
want to be ....

THE FIRST EARTH BATTALION

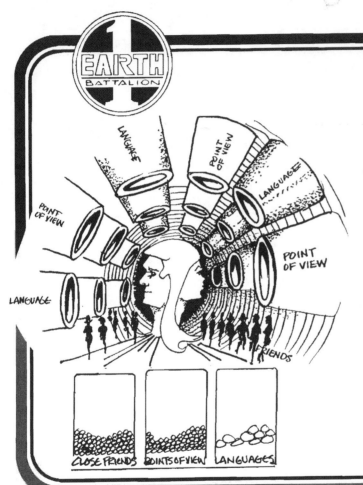

LANGUAGE
POINT OF VIEW
LANGUAGE
POINT OF VIEW
POINT OF VIEW
LANGUAGE
FRIENDS

CLOSE FRIENDS　POINTS OF VIEW　LANGUAGES

Some of the things we do on this world have survival value. That is, certain acquisitions appear to have more value in afterlife than others. It is speculation, of course, but many 'belief systems' have similar notions about what you can take with you. Many anticipate afterlife wherein you are with all the good friends you made. Points of view and languages directly contribute to the number of ways you can know something. Both contribute to Universal intelligence. What counts? Knowing what GOD knows is getting more like GOD.

THE FIRST EARTH BATTALION

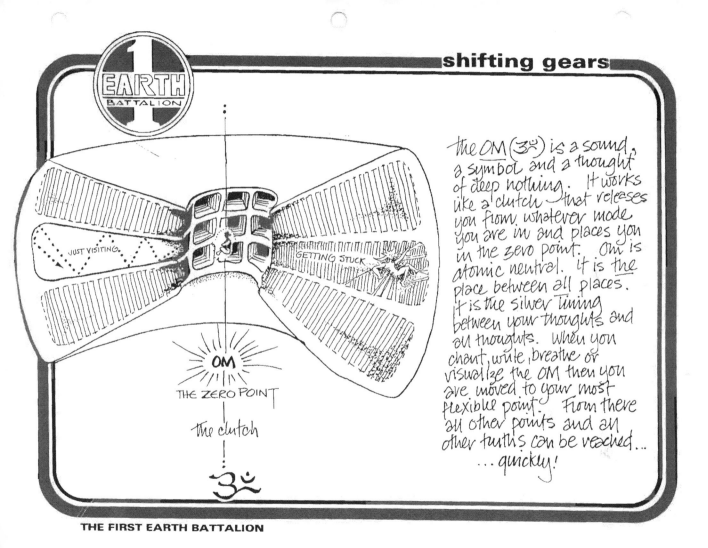

the OM (ॐ) is a sound, a symbol and a thought of deep nothing. It works like a clutch that releases you from whatever mode you are in and places you in the zero point. OM is atomic neutral. It is the place between all places. It is the silver lining between your thoughts and all thoughts. When you chant, write, breathe or visualize the OM then you are moved to your most flexible point. From there all other points and all other truths can be reached...
...quickly!

JUST VISITING.

GETTING STUCK

OM
THE ZERO POINT

the clutch

ॐ

THE FIRST EARTH BATTALION

1 EARTH BATTALION

SOME ARE RULED BY RULES... THEY WANT A FORMULA TO GO BY. THEY ARE EFFICIENT AND SERVE BUT THEY ARE NOT FREE...

THE WARRIOR MONK UNDERSTANDS THE VALUE OF DISCIPLINE TO FREE TIME FOR SERVICE

BUT (S)HE IS OPEN AND CAN SEE OPPORTUNITIES TO "TASTE" LIFE AS (S)HE GOES ABOUT THE TASK OF SERVICE.

OTHERS ARE FREE.. BUT HAVING NO ORDER THEY GET LITTLE DONE FOR OTHERS. THE MUNDANE IN THEIR LIFE TENDS TO CONSUME THEM...THEY CANNOT SERVE.

THE FIRST EARTH BATTALION

Freedom comes from having the mundane everyday activities in your world packaged into a tight pattern of _order_. It doesn't mean you should be in a mechanical stupor when you're doing them... It is good to _taste_ the _moment_ in everything your up to... but don't let the routine of life consume your day. Organize your personal work into a pattern, thereby powering up the time left for planetary service.

EARTH 1 BATTALION

- ⊙ TAI CHI
- • MO GAI
- • NINJITSU
- • TSIN HZUEH POINTS
- ⊙ AI KI DO
- • PA KUA SHING YI
- • SHAOLIN
- • SOFT STYLE KARATE
- • WU SHU KUNG FU
- • HARD STYLE KARATE
- • CHINESE BOXING
- • TUMBLING

FOR ALL DECISION-MAKERS / OTHERS
> The internal styles for calm

FOR STRATEGISTS
> The indirect or circular styles

FOR JR. LEADERS
> The tactical styles

FOR FIGHTERS
> The direct styles

(axes: ALL BODIES · SPIRITUAL · HEALTH · FINESSE · INTERNAL POWER / STRONG BODIES · TACTICAL · STRENGTH · BRUTE FORCE · EXTERNAL POWER)

In the end the Martial Arts serve only one real function .. and that is to open the warrior up to the truth. Achieving control and self-confidence allow the warrior to trust the system ... and it is then the spirit can come in. But there are some practical applications of the system as well and you should make a conscious selection based on need and capability.

⊙ QUALITY OF INSTRUCTION USUALLY BASED ON SPIRITUAL ABILITIES OF THE SCHOOL AND MASTER.

⊙ EARTH BATTALION MEMBERS SHOULD FOCUS ON THE MOST SPIRITUALLY ORIENTED FORMS OF AI KI DO AND TAI CHI.

THE FIRST EARTH BATTALION

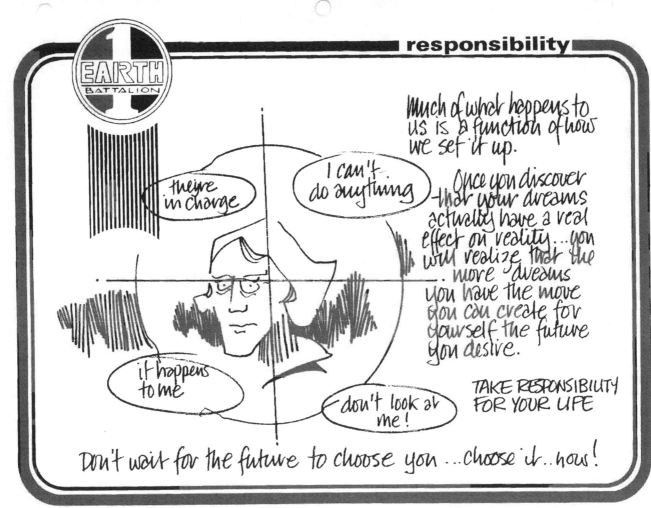

Organizational structures often get like the dinosaur... their bodies become too big for their little mouths to feed. Management overhead, stagnant communications systems eventually topple the turkey. If however you have an early experience like a vietnam or a watergate...the more alert begin to look for a new operating style based on projected values and high powered mythology.

THIS IS HOW A FIRST EARTH BATTALION CAN HELP!

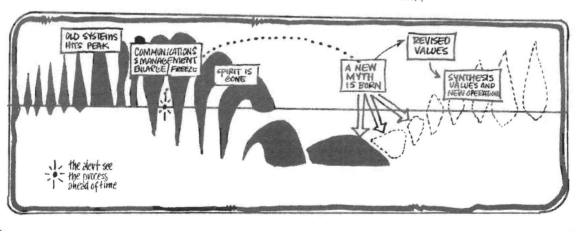

OLD SYSTEMS HITS PEAK

COMMUNICATIONS & MANAGEMENT ENLARGE FREEZE

SPIRIT IS GONE

A NEW MYTH IS BORN

REVISED VALUES

SYNTHESIS VALUES AND NEW OPERATION

the alert see the process ahead of time

THE FIRST EARTH BATTALION

THE FIRST EARTH BATTALION

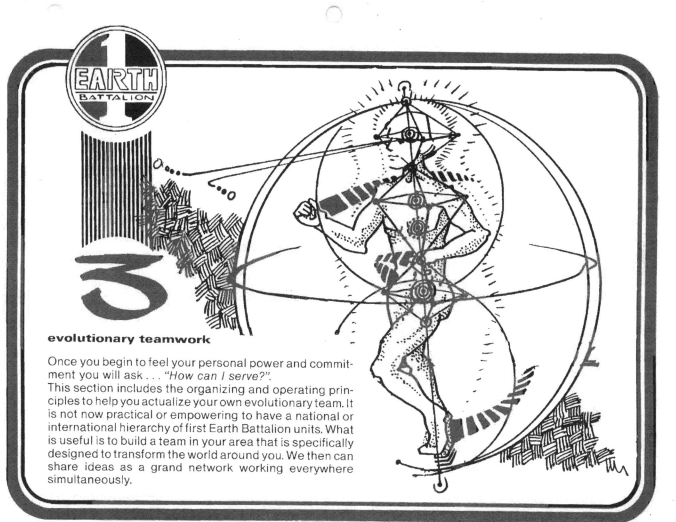

evolutionary teamwork

Once you begin to feel your personal power and commitment you will ask . . . *"How can I serve?"*.

This section includes the organizing and operating principles to help you actualize your own evolutionary team. It is not now practical or empowering to have a national or international hierarchy of first Earth Battalion units. What is useful is to build a team in your area that is specifically designed to transform the world around you. We then can share ideas as a grand network working everywhere simultaneously.

THE FIRST EARTH BATTALION

Well, the old rules and models for generating a large organizational structure just didn't seem an appropriate way to harness this new age enthusiasm. One thing that did surface however was that most of the individuals who continuously practiced and were satisfied with evolutionary work were organized in small autonomous groups of close friends. The other organizational development that had power was the network. Since the most powerful resource in the post-industrial world is information . . . the structure that best delivers and organizes information sources is the network.

So, what we are proposing is that if pursuing the Earth Battalion work is exciting to you, then organize your own small group following the suggested steps enclosed. Match the organization to the needs of your community and the personal development needs of your members. Use the First Earth Battalion name, as it empowers your group. When you are organized and operating . . . check back into the network with us and we'll generate some schemes that involve national and international action. Whether you connect into the international network right away is not significant. Think about what level of commitment your team could make when employed for a national concern. Can they leave town? For how many days? To do something physical? We'll let you know about the coordinating developments as they pop.

Use the attached ideas but be creative and enjoy the work and pleasure associated with your own continued growth and enlightened action.

evolutionary teamwork

In recent years there have been some very exciting evolutionary ideas put forward. One confounding factor was that the authors of these ideas were not prepared to organize the enthusiasm generated by their work. The common plea from the readers was "How can we serve?".

THE FIRST EARTH BATTALION

EARTH BATTALION 1

making time for good work

On EARTH DAY we spend our time working for PEOPLE AND PLANET. Those of a generation that helped cover the land with concrete . . . then begin to cover the concrete with plants . . . they can live togther with some design and care. Let the young, who haven't yet begun to worry about environment . . . plant one or more trees. These trees can be their investment in a green future. Other larger organizations can replant and refurbish the forests grown up during their lifetimes.

It isn't true that only pure nature can grow the most beautiful habitats. People can consciously design and organize nature in a far superior way. Everyone's neighborhood can be a lush garden with the capability to feed the caretakers in times of need.

If we believe in things like peace and taking care of the earth, then we must resource them accordingly. If peace is as important as collecting weapons for national defense, them we must resource peace with the same emphasis.

Since everybody can't insert themselves into an active role in peacemaking every week, we might consider something we can do . . . like take care of mother earth. Since the national work force is looking at a four day week, why not make fridays . . . EARTH DAY.

That could also be the day that your group met to improve themselves as individuals. A morning of work on the habitat and an afternoon working on self and group.

PEOPLE AND PLANET

benevolent commando raids

radio is the peoples friend

Conducting high consciousness commando raids may be confusing to some so here is an example:

CREATING GUERRILLA GURUS . . . .

The most powerful dynamic you can get operating is an independent agent who continues to do transformational work and furthermore generates that same instinct in others. This is called auto-catalytic.

THE CONSPIRACY OF SPARKLING EYES
PHASE 1. Get your team or any large group together. Have them return home and call one or more DJ's in town. Have them report with various kinds of apparent confusion and amazement that "Peoples' eyes are changing . . . somehow beginning to sparkle". They can say that if you stare deeply into someone's eyes near you that you can see an inner light. The IDEA of course is to begin to allow people to appreciate each other's essence by increasing the intensity of eye contact.

PHASE II. The same people call again two weeks later in greater intervals and report: "We have finally discovered how to tell which people got the sparkly eyes first . . . and they can be spotted because they're the ones who automatically hug you upon greeting . . . etc . . . etc.

NOW BE CREATIVE AND GENERATE
SOME MORE OF THE SAME

THE FIRST EARTH BATTALION

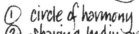

team meeting

1. circle of harmony
2. sharing indiv. progress
3. alternating reading
4. team plans
5. group fun
6. closing aspirations

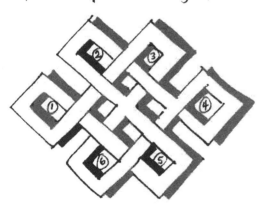

The FIRST EARTH BATTALION is a grassroots idea. If it doesn't move you to some local team-building action then it isn't ready yet. If it does move you then don't ask to be spoon fed. Put a small team together and begin the WORK.

Mix a program of studying this manual and the related books recommended herein. Discuss things openly and develop a way for the group to pray or otherwise tune in to its higher self. Meet once a week. Begin by working on getting yourself awake, physically smoothed out and eating properly. The rest will follow. Sharing the ways you are improving makes for great group discussion material. Consider the lotus for your own personal program and the arrowed path as the sequence for the group work to follow. Read and discuss the books suggested. Do the trainings suggested if they are convenient to your area.

Once the team feels together and can agree on a benevolent service project, then begin to conduct benevolent raids in order to wake up your community to the truth. We can cooperate with each other, the biosphere and the universe if we choose to.

A circle of harmony is recommended to open and close the meetings. The specific way you do it is unimportant as long as there is a joining of hands and some silence. Right palm over left seems to generate a directional flow within the circle. The process unites the group with each other and the universe. GOOD HUNTING!!

THE FIRST EARTH BATTALION

making family

ACTION: THE CIRCLE OF HARMONY

It's important to create unity for our transformational
work. It is a Universal truth that we are all one and
can call upon our higher selves if we choose to.
The technology of unity appears complex,
but is only a collection of very simple
sense linking steps.

In order to feel as if you are one with
your team, then all of your collective
senses must be aligned. This is called
sensory synch.

The eyes can be focused with a candle
or guided imagery. The ears are best
aligned with music that is repetitive in
sound and phrase. Likewise each of the
other senses is given a powerful and unique
stimulus until everyone in the group absolutely
feels as if they are one. They will in this case each be
experiencing exactly the same sensory input for all
their senses. The effect is exciting and spiritually
comforting.

TAKING TIME OUT TO TUNE IN

THE FIRST EARTH BATTALION

mother Earth... my life support system..
as a soldier.. I must drink your blue
water.. live inside your red clay and
eat your green skin__.
I pray.... my boots will always kiss
your face and my footsteps match
your heartbeat...

carry my body thru space and time...
you are my connection to the
Universe...and all that comes after.
I am yours and you are mine
I salute you__

THE FIRST EARTH BATTALION

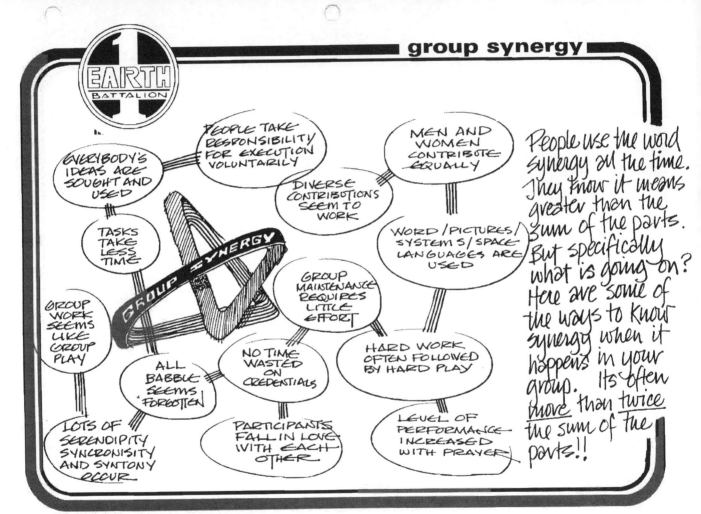

EARTH 1 BATTALION

EVERYBODY'S IDEAS ARE SOUGHT AND USED

PEOPLE TAKE RESPONSIBILITY FOR EXECUTION VOLUNTARILY

MEN AND WOMEN CONTRIBUTE EQUALLY

DIVERSE CONTRIBUTIONS SEEM TO WORK

TASKS TAKE LESS TIME

WORD/PICTURES/SYSTEMS/SPACE LANGUAGES ARE USED

GROUP SYNERGY

GROUP MAINTENANCE REQUIRES LITTLE EFFORT

GROUP WORK SEEMS LIKE GROUP PLAY

NO TIME WASTED ON CREDENTIALS

HARD WORK OFTEN FOLLOWED BY HARD PLAY

ALL BABBLE SEEMS FORGOTTEN

LOTS OF SERENDIPITY SYNCRONISITY AND SYNTONY OCCUR

PARTICIPANTS FALL IN LOVE WITH EACH OTHER

LEVEL OF PERFORMANCE INCREASED WITH PRAYER

People use the word synergy all the time. They know it means greater than the sum of the parts. But specifically what is going on? Here are some of the ways to know synergy when it happens in your group. Its often _more_ than _twice_ the sum of the parts!!

THE FIRST EARTH BATTALION

1 EARTH BATTALION

identify your team with the other planetary workers!

ACTION: SYMBOL LINKING

There are a set of emerging symbols that can unify all the forces on the planet who are in an evolutionary mode. These windows on the transformational process can more quickly unify global consciousness if we can agree to use them whenever and wherever we can.

VISUAL SPECTRUM   Symbols, flags, colors

EARTH RISE   RAINBOW

OLIVE WREATH   PYRAMID

colors in the ultra tones
turqoise
violet
magenta

· any logo can be blended with one of these symbols

AUDIO SPECTRUM   Hymns, salutations, chants

anthem

Johann Pachelbel's canon in D

music in the heart range

country music

the salutations
om shanti
shalom
Namaste

affirmations
Rah!
Ho!

chants
Om Namah Shivaya
Toham Kum Rah
alleluya

sounds in the AH and OM vibration open the mind and the heart

Recognize that, there are symbols & signs that already unify new world thinking.

the mystics in many ways were spiritual engineers.

symbols, sounds & colors have specific emotional effects.

Begin to listen to the lyrics in popular songs... you will find all the lessons for transformation are here.

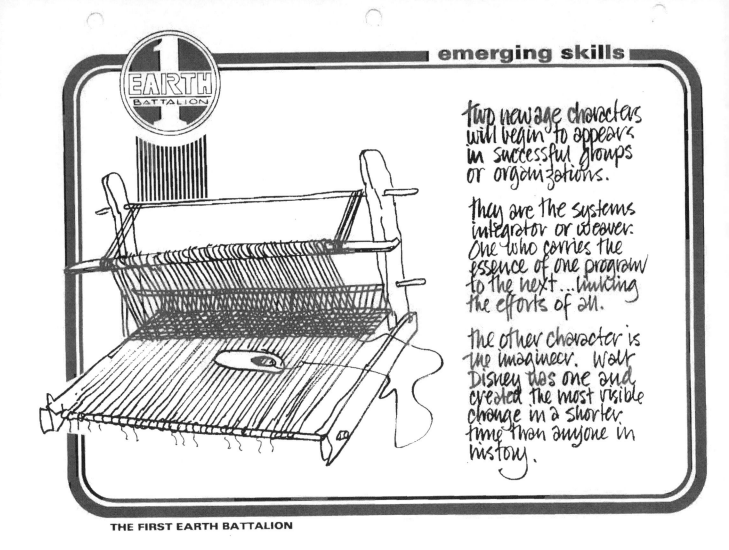

two new age characters will begin to appears in successful groups or organizations.

they are the systems integrator or weaver. one who carries the essence of one program to the next...linking the efforts of all.

the other character is the imagineer. walt Disney was one and created the most visible change in a shorter time than anyone in history.

THE FIRST EARTH BATTALION

One of the grandest moments in personal development trainings is to watch people "pop out of the jelly" caught out of their lives in a set of belief systems that have blocked them from realizing we are all one family ...... often zeroing experience like warfare ... or a truly loving group of friends that causes people to realize they are CONNECTED to all of those around them in a deep & profound way.

this is the planets newest spectator sport...
CONSCIOUSNESS WORK

THE FIRST EARTH BATTALION

CAPACITIES :
MEDITATION
LOCAL WORK
ON THE ROAD
TOTAL DEDICATION

NETWORKS

connecting the teams.......

PHASE I. Locate/address/catagorize the community

PHASE I. Locate/address/catagorize the community organizations in your region. Have a way to call or communicate with each.

PHASE II. Determine the kinds of service each can perform. Some groups may only be able to meditate on an idea, others may be able to pack up and work on a dam project out of town for a week. Get the catagories clarified.

PHASE III. Use the network to share information of importance to the community.

PHASE IV. Activate grand networks with regional tasks of interest to all. Do this on friday.

Should a serious problem like an earthquake or financial crash effect your region . . . this kind of community cohesion would drastically reduce the chaos and generate the structure for recovery.

A NATIONAL OPERATIONS CENTER FOR WORLD NETWORKING AWAITS MAJOR FUNDING

THE FIRST EARTH BATTALION

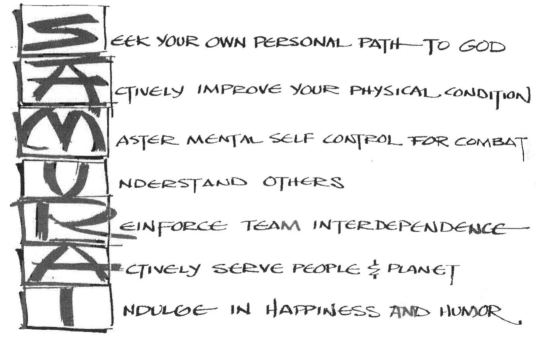

SEEK YOUR OWN PERSONAL PATH TO GOD

ACTIVELY IMPROVE YOUR PHYSICAL CONDITION

MASTER MENTAL SELF CONTROL FOR COMBAT

UNDERSTAND OTHERS

REINFORCE TEAM INTERDEPENDENCE

ACTIVELY SERVE PEOPLE & PLANET

INDULGE IN HAPPINESS AND HUMOR.

THE FIRST EARTH BATTALION

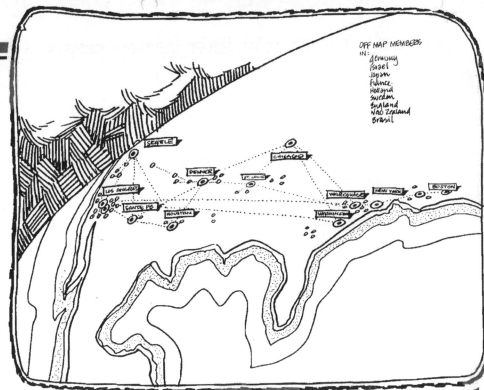

OFF MAP MEMBERS
IN:
Germany
Israel
Japan
France
Holland
Sweden
England
New Zealand
Brasil

SEATTLE
DENVER
CHICAGO
LOS ANGELES
ST. LOUIS
SANTA FE
HOUSTON
WAR COLLEGE
NEW YORK
BOSTON
WASHINGTON

Over 1000
warriors and
warriors friends
share a network
of ideas and
transformational
schemes.

the FIRST EARTH BATTALION is structured as an information network.

the network

THE FIRST EARTH BATTALION

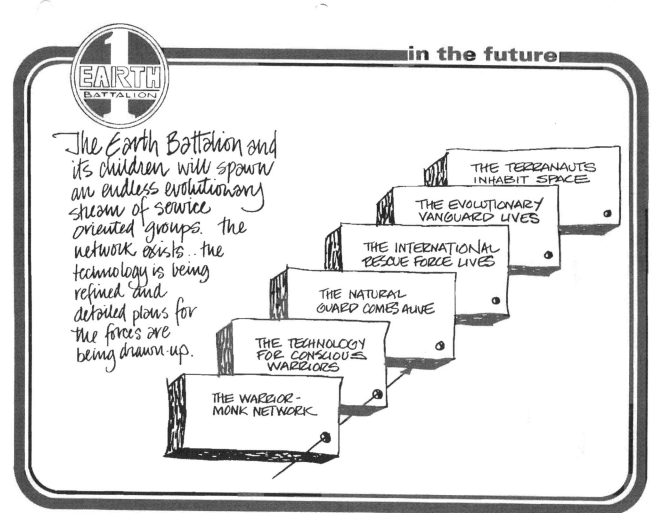

The Earth Battalion and its children will spawn an endless evolutionary stream of service oriented groups. the network exists.. the technology is being refined and detailed plans for the forces are being drawn-up.

THE TERRANAUTS INHABIT SPACE

THE EVOLUTIONARY VANGUARD LIVES

THE INTERNATIONAL RESCUE FORCE LIVES

THE NATURAL GUARD COMES ALIVE

THE TECHNOLOGY FOR CONSCIOUS WARRIORS

THE WARRIOR-MONK NETWORK

THE FIRST EARTH BATTALION

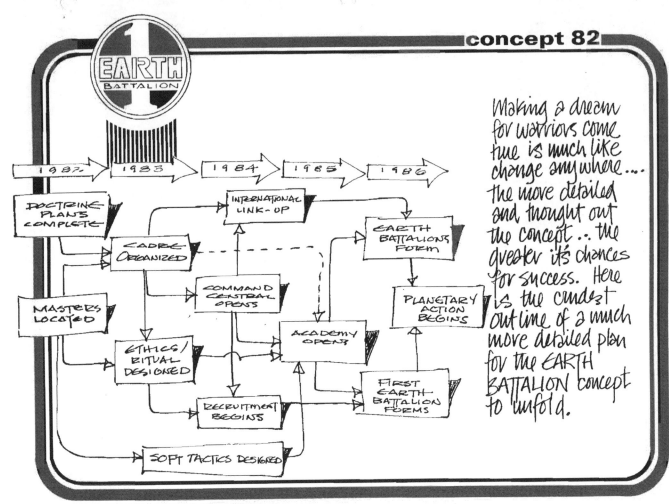

1
EARTH
BATTALION

1982   1983   1984   1985   1986

DOCTRINE
PLANS
COMPLETE

INTERNATIONAL
LINK-UP

CADRE
ORGANIZED

EARTH
BATTALIONS
FORM

MASTERS
LOCATED

COMMAND
CENTRAL
OPENS

PLANETARY
ACTION
BEGINS

ACADEMY
OPENS

ETHICS/
RITUAL
DESIGNED

FIRST
EARTH
BATTALION
FORMS

RECRUITMENT
BEGINS

SOFT TACTICS DESIGNED

Making a dream
for warriors come
true is much like
change anywhere...
the more detailed
and thought out
the concept .·. the
greater it's chances
for success. Here
is the crudest
outline of a much
more detailed plan
for the EARTH
BATTALION concept
to unfold.

THE FIRST EARTH BATTALION

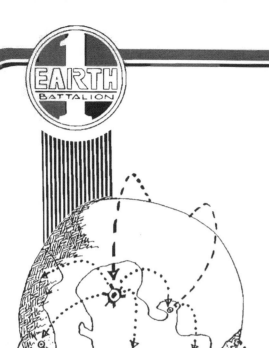

A primary function of the FIRST EARTH is to communicate ideas. Set up a network of information within your army and with friends in any army. Soon continental co-ordinators will emerge and then we will consider communications media other than the mail and telephone.

Let this battalion grow _wherever_ there is interest.

THE FIRST EARTH BATTALION

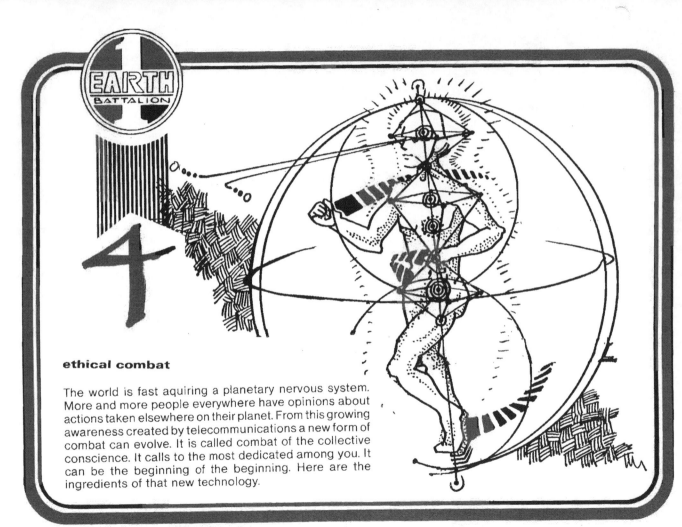

ethical combat

The world is fast aquiring a planetary nervous system. More and more people everywhere have opinions about actions taken elsewhere on their planet. From this growing awareness created by telecommunications a new form of combat can evolve. It is called combat of the collective conscience. It calls to the most dedicated among you. It can be the beginning of the beginning. Here are the ingredients of that new technology.

THE FIRST EARTH BATTALION

ethical combat

Some critical events have occurred that have dramatically shifted the working dynamics of combat. These events and the advance of technical communications combine to create new criteria for winning and losing. Nations and armies that ignore the new ingredients for victory will suffer strange defeats which may grant them the battle but lose them the war.

During a critical moment in the war in Vietnam the world was exposed to the cold-blooded execution of a Viet Cong terrorist by a senior South Vietnamese government official. The news photo and film of this official firing a pistol point-blank into head of the terrorist flashed around the world to an excess of four hundred million people. No explanation could change the visceral and emotional reaction of the world. The South Vietnamese lost that war.

Recently a conflict involving Samoza's regime in Nicaruagua was dramatically changed by an internationally broadcasted killing. A newsman under live camera coverage bellied up to a mamber of Samoza's army and was shot to death in an apparently non-sensical way. The world watched. Samoza's government fell the next day.

The world with its elaborate international network of interconnected news systems has become a planetary nervous system. Hundreds of millions of people watch the camera-worthy events of any conflict wherein the camera is present. Also, humans all seem to manifest primary gut level reactions to unethical action. Put these elements together and you have established a new style of warfare. We call it the combat of the collective conscience. This combat projects the winning force as one which executes the more ethical action in the face of accompanying cameras. This changes the alternatives to force projection. It portends non-violent combat. It expands the boundaries of action and reaction.

Stategic objectives now include protecting cities. Tactical actions now include the projection of love and concern. The door is opened for joint US and Soviet cooperation.

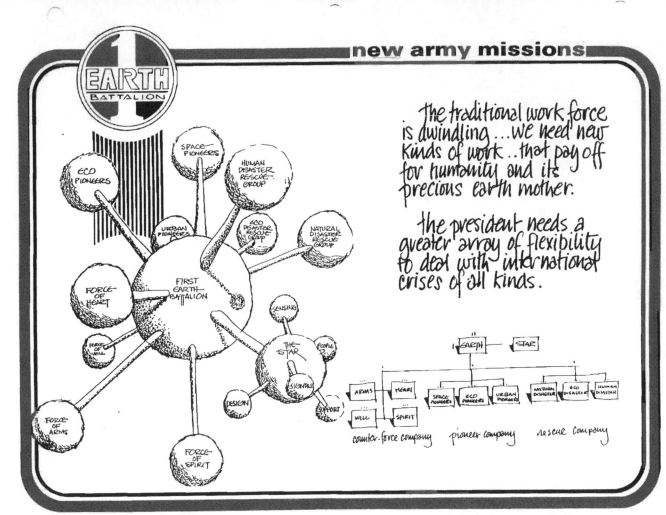

the traditional work force is dwindling...we need new kinds of work...that pay off for humanity and its precious earth mother.

the president needs a greater array of flexibility to deal with international crises of all kinds.

THE FIRST EARTH BATTALION

Here are many new kinds of responses to old and emerging world problems... why not try them?

CONFLICT	NORMAL RESPONSE BY MILITARY UNIT	SOFT TACTICS RESPONSE	RESPONSIBLE TEAM
HOSTAGES... iran type situation	high risk	one for one exchange earth bn w/hostages	COUNTER FORCE — TM HEART
FANATICS, capture of Holy Monument	high risk	counter demonstration organized by earth bn.	COUNTER FORCE — TM SPIRIT
AFGHAN, type invasion imminent	little national interest... no action	unit lines up on border under television camera	COUNTERFORCE — TM WILL
HOSTAGES... for mercenary reasons	commando strike (if politically feasible)	same but with world sanction	COUNTERFORCE — TM ARMS
ENERGY CRISIS	takes normal conservation steps	builds ecologically solvent community	PIONEER TEAM ECO
URBAN BLIGHT with looting chaos	National guard security and crime control	join intercity population for solution	PIONEER TEAM URBAN
NOTIFIED OF UNEXPLAINED EXTRA TERRESTRIAL LANDING	none planned	set up landing area & language system	PIONEER TEAM SPACE
OIL SPILL IN LOW population beach area	not enough outcry to help!	team begins work to protect biosphere	RESCUE TEAM BIO DISASTER
EARTHQUAKE... FLOOD etc.	National guard assistance	organizes local people into teams	RESCUE TEAM NATURAL DISASTER
HUMAN TRAGEDY.... Cambodian genocide	none	organizes popular emergency relief	RESCUE TEAM HUMAN DISASTER

THE FIRST EARTH BATTALION

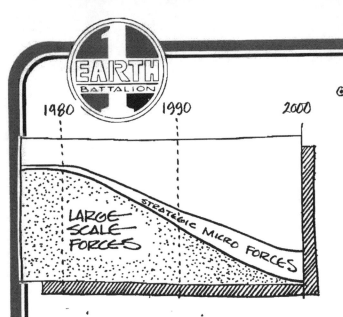

1980   1990   2000

LARGE SCALE FORCES

STRATEGIC MICRO FORCES

The day most of the world watched war on television they all helped decide who won...... and from that point on conflicts were decided based on who had the most RIGHT not the most MIGHT.

The day nuclear weapons were considered for use during the early moments of a conflict then the need for mass armies disappeared.

The day terrorists discovered television and mass news coverage they committed large scale acts with small scale forces and the need for strategic Micro action arrived.

THE FIRST EARTH BATTALION

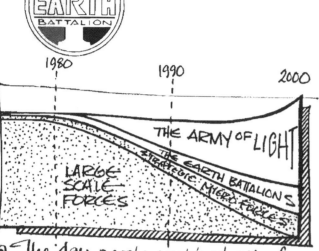

1980   1990   2000

THE ARMY OF LIGHT

THE EARTH BATTALION'S
STRATEGIC MICRO FORCES

LARGE
SCALE
FORCES

⊙ The day most people realized the EARTH was still plagued with the injustice of tyrants......

⊙ The day most people realized the EARTH was racked with pollution......

⊙ The day most people realized natural disasters were more disasterous for some people than others...

then the need for SERVICE FORCES came .. at last.

⊙ The day people realized all of the believers and caring beings had to come together to work as warriors ... then came the day for the FORCES OF LIGHT to unite!

CONVENTIONAL RESPONSE

THE ALLIES MUST REALIZE THAT THE PRINCIPLES OF WAR THAT APPLIED TO THE LARGER FORCE MUST NOW BE MODIFIED FOR THE SMALLER ALLIED FORCES.

NUCLEAR TRIPWIRE

SINCE NUCLEAR RESPONSE IS BECOMING AN EXPECTED EARLY RESPONSE TO OVERT ATTACK THE BULK OF CONVENTIONAL FORCES CAN BE REPLACED BY BORDERLINE FORCES.

STRATEGIC MICROACTION

THE CONFLICTS REQUIRING ACTIONS ARE SMALLER AFFAIRS PROPELLED BY TELEVISION. THE SOLUTION MUST BE DEFT, FAST AND CAMERA WORTHY.

A major shift in the criterion for victory has already begun. Since the advent of worldwide television coverage, the judgements for success in battle have changed. Victory will now accrue to the force that executes an action most consistent with evolving world values. Destroying your opponent and his property will in the long run equal defeat.

THE FIRST EARTH BATTALION

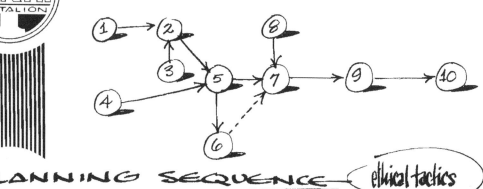

PLANNING SEQUENCE — ethical tactics

(1) SECURE MEDIA CONNECTION

(2) PLAN PHASES OF INTERVENTION

(3) USE INDIGENOUS PLANNER

(4) SECURE HUMANITARIAN ENDORSEMENT

(5) MAKE PLAN

(6) SIMULATE .. CHECK 2d/3d ORDER EFFECTS

(7) REHEARSE WITH ANTICIPATED COUNTERS

(8) PRETAPE EVENT IN CASE OF CAPTURE

(9) PRACTICE / PRACTICE

(10) EXECUTE THE TACTIC

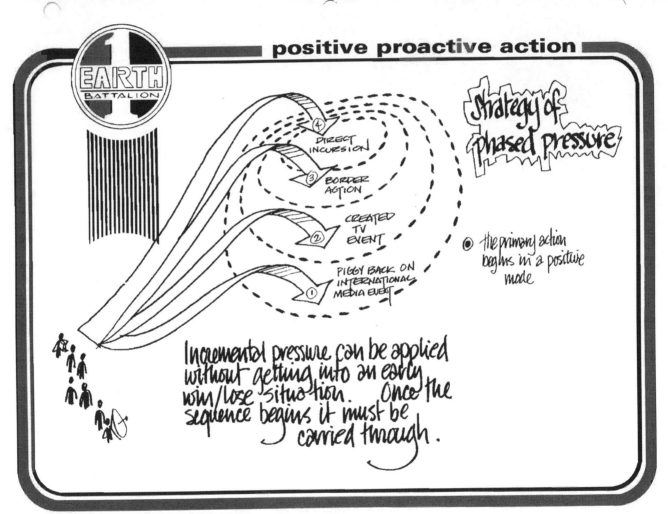

1 EARTH BATTALION

Strategy of phased Pressure

④ DIRECT INCURSION

③ BORDER ACTION

② CREATED TV EVENT

① PIGGY BACK ON INTERNATIONAL MEDIA EVENT

⦿ the primary action begins in a positive mode

Incremental pressure can be applied without getting into an early win/lose situation. Once the sequence begins it must be carried through.

THE FIRST EARTH BATTALION

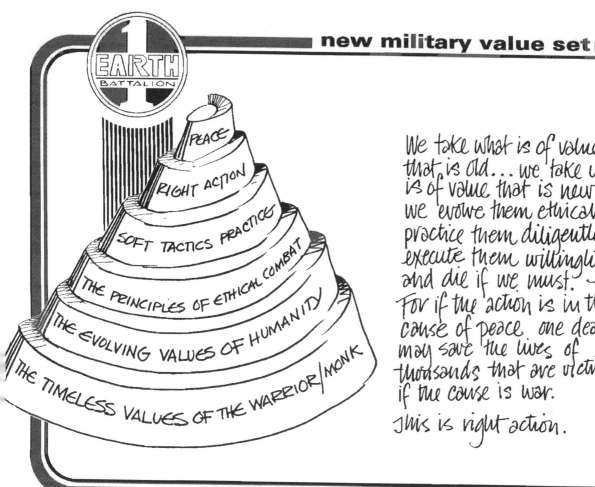

EARTH
BATTALION
1

PEACE

RIGHT ACTION

SOFT TACTICS PRACTICE

THE PRINCIPLES OF ETHICAL COMBAT

THE EVOLVING VALUES OF HUMANITY

THE TIMELESS VALUES OF THE WARRIOR/MONK

We take what is of value that is old... we take what is of value that is new... we evolve them ethically.. practice them diligently.. execute them willingly.. and die if we must. For if the action is in the cause of peace one death may save the lives of thousands that are victims if the cause is war.

This is right action.

THE FIRST EARTH BATTALION

1 EARTH BATTALION

ETHICAL COMBAT

Any Earth battalion member that suits up for combat before the camera's will bear the flag of their country on one sleeve and the symbol of their religion or belief system on the other sleeve. the unit member from the country in question uses a loudspeaker (given to all battalion members) to talk the battalion thru the population of any country.

THE FIRST EARTH BATTALION

EARTH
1
BATTALION

indigenous music
and words of peace

county
flags
&
spiritual
symbols

the battalion
carries the
symbols and
sounds of
peace

symbolic flowers

symbolic
animal

THE FIRST EARTH BATTALION

1 EARTH BATTALION

typical battle scenario FIRST EARTH

they parachuted in that morning and stood in two lines facing each opposing army. the EARTH BATTALION. satellite above...beamed this image to the globe. the EARTH watched as this potential catastrophy awaited the conscience of one or both of the commanders to act. For they would have to bloody the EARTH BATTALION people in their path before they could attack...
...and the world would know who started it!

THE FIRST EARTH BATTALION

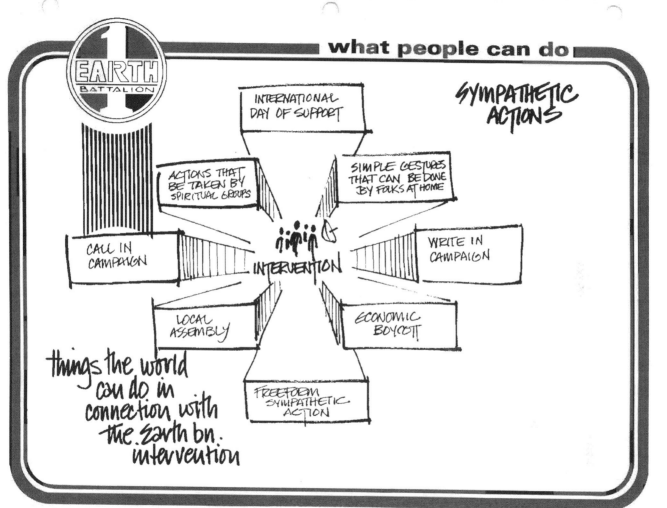

Warfare currently comprises about 16 dimensions. In 1990 there will be 5 new additions... or five new areas the tax payers must bear..... or five new possible ways for the ultimate conflict to be triggered.

the five new dimensions are:

- directed energy weapons

- space based platforms

- nuclear terrorism

- changed public awareness

- changed international collective conscience

We need to WORK THESE DIMENSIONS NOW before they begin to work against us!

1990 ENVIRONMENT

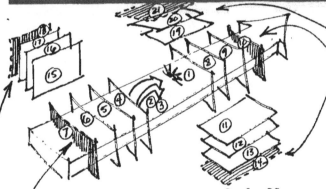

multi-dimensional challenges

THE FIRST EARTH BATTALION

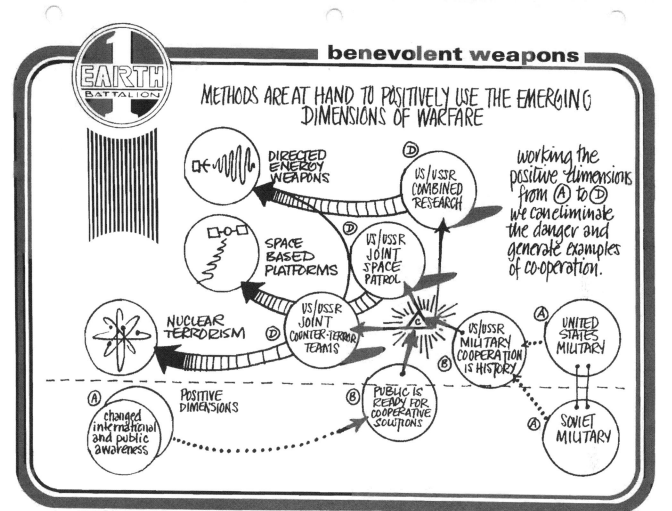

METHODS ARE AT HAND TO POSITIVELY USE THE EMERGING DIMENSIONS OF WARFARE

DIRECTED ENERGY WEAPONS

Ⓓ US/USSR COMBINED RESEARCH

Ⓓ US/USSR JOINT SPACE PATROL

SPACE BASED PLATFORMS

NUCLEAR TERRORISM

Ⓓ US/USSR JOINT COUNTER-TERROR TEAMS

c

US/USSR MILITARY COOPERATION IS HISTORY

Ⓐ UNITED STATES MILITARY

Ⓑ

working the positive dimensions from Ⓐ to Ⓓ we can eliminate the danger and generate examples of co-operation.

Ⓐ SOVIET MILITARY

Ⓐ POSITIVE DIMENSIONS

changed international and public awareness

Ⓑ PUBLIC IS READY FOR COOPERATIVE SOLUTIONS

THE FIRST EARTH BATTALION

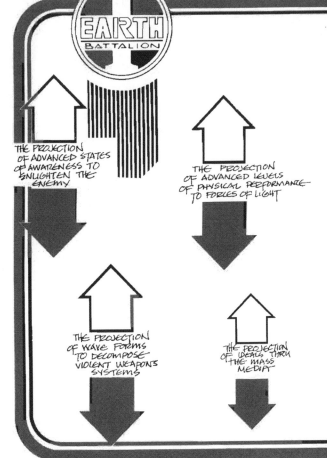

THE PROJECTION OF ADVANCED STATES OF AWARENESS TO ENLIGHTEN THE ENEMY

THE PROJECTION OF ADVANCED LEVELS OF PHYSICAL PERFORMANCE TO FORCES OF LIGHT

THE PROJECTION OF WAVE FORMS TO DECOMPOSE VIOLENT WEAPONS SYSTEMS

THE PROJECTION OF IDEALS THRU THE MASS MEDIA

If you look for clear examples of where the free world has an advantage over the world of non-believers you will discover two resources that clearly stand out in our favor. They are GOD and micro electronics. The beauty in that is you can use the micro electronics to project the spirit.... Brains work like that. Hence the field of psycho electronic weaponry.

THE FIRST EARTH BATTALION

1 EARTH BATTALION

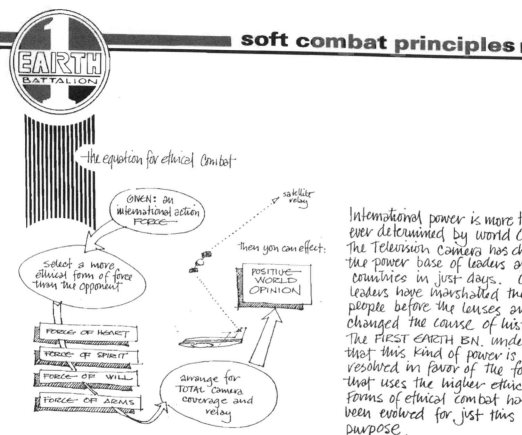

the equation for ethical combat

GIVEN: an international action FORCE

select a more ethical form of force than the opponent

FORCE OF HEART
FORCE OF SPIRIT
FORCE OF WILL
FORCE OF ARMS

arrange for TOTAL camera coverage and relay

satellite relay

then you can effect:

POSITIVE WORLD OPINION

International power is more than ever determined by world opinion. The Television camera has changed the power base of leaders and countries in just days. Clever leaders have marshalled their people before the lenses and changed the course of history. The FIRST EARTH BN. understands that this kind of power is resolved in favor of the force that uses the higher ethic. Forms of ethical combat have been evolved for just this purpose.

THE FIRST EARTH BATTALION

1 EARTH BATTALION

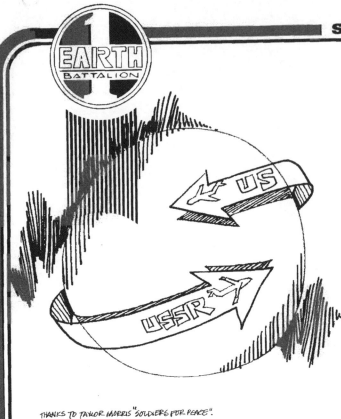

THANKS TO TAYLOR MORRIS "SOLDIERS FOR PEACE".

systematically defuzing the planet has proven difficult...but almost overnight a contingent of soldiers and their families could be exchanged between the soviet union and the united states.

they would live, and work and serve as a constant reminder to any party tempted to take nuclear advantage of the other.

Yes, there are many creative options other than the arms race.....whose in charge of creating those options?

THE FIRST EARTH BATTALION

In the martial arts, one learns a number of possible counter moves against different types of possible enemies. These practice battles are done over and over until they become instinct. Likewise in the EARTH BATTALION all plausible engagements are war-gamed until each soldier has the routine cold. In this way the battalion can operate in the absence of commands from its leaders, who may be out of touch, because of the new realities of modern warfare.

THE FIRST EARTH BATTALION

connecting an army of light

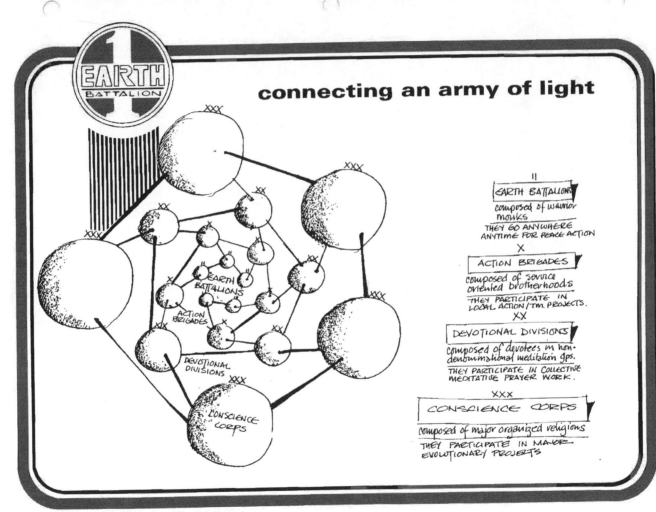

EARTH BATTALIONS
composed of warrior monks
THEY GO ANYWHERE ANYTIME FOR PEACE ACTION

X

ACTION BRIGADES
composed of service oriented brotherhoods
THEY PARTICIPATE IN LOCAL ACTION / T.M. PROJECTS.

XX

DEVOTIONAL DIVISIONS
composed of devotees in non-denominational meditation gps.
THEY PARTICIPATE IN COLLECTIVE MEDITATIVE PRAYER WORK.

XXX

CONSCIENCE CORPS
composed of major organized religions
THEY PARTICIPATE IN MAJOR EVOLUTIONARY PROJECTS

THE FIRST EARTH BATTALION

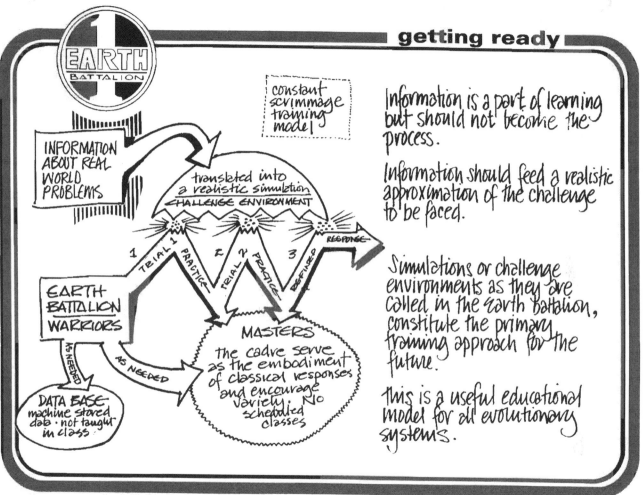

EARTH 1 BATTALION

constant scrimmage training model

INFORMATION ABOUT REAL WORLD PROBLEMS

translated into a realistic simulation
CHALLENGE ENVIRONMENT

1 TRIAL 1 PRACTICE 2 TRIAL 2 PRACTICE 3 REFINED RESPONSE

EARTH BATTALION WARRIORS

AS NEEDED

AS NEEDED

DATA BASE machine stored data · not taught in class

MASTERS
the cadre serve as the embodiment of classical responses and encourage variety. No scheduled classes

Information is a part of learning but should not become the process.

Information should feed a realistic approximation of the challenge to be faced.

Simulations or challenge environments as they are called in the Earth Battalion, constitute the primary training approach for the future.

This is a useful educational model for all evolutionary systems.

THE FIRST EARTH BATTALION

1 EARTH BATTALION

Dwight Eisenhower said:

"Someday people are going to want peace so badly that the governments of the world will have to stand back and let them have it"

Someday the soldiers of the world may come to their highest ideals and realize that only they can agree to disarm the world time bomb.

THE FIRST EARTH BATTALION

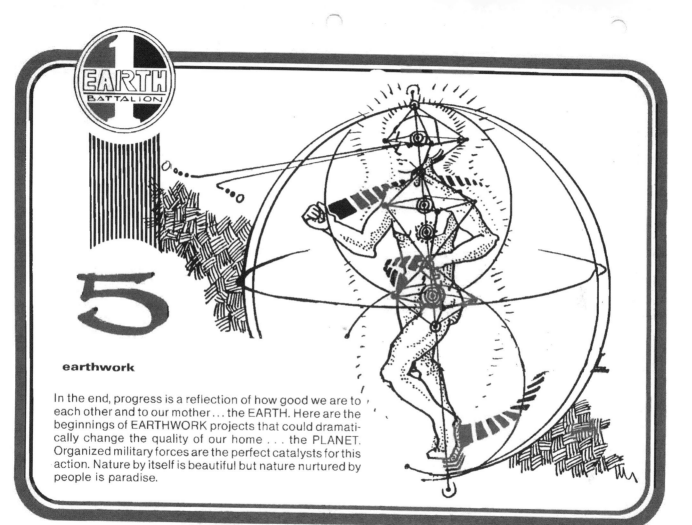

1 EARTH BATTALION

5

earthwork

In the end, progress is a reflection of how good we are to each other and to our mother ... the EARTH. Here are the beginnings of EARTHWORK projects that could dramatically change the quality of our home ... the PLANET. Organized military forces are the perfect catalysts for this action. Nature by itself is beautiful but nature nurtured by people is paradise.

THE FIRST EARTH BATTALION

Natural wilderness is wonderful, but can't really compare with the result when man consciously organizes and nurtures the plants and waterways. The lack of care and attention paid to our mother earth is criminal compared with the results that could be forthcoming with a massive organized effort.

Armies have traditionally served as evolutionary agents in organizing and training nature. West Point was established to train military civil engineers. The Corps of Engineers today manages the nation's waterways. The work of massive reforestation for example is a natural for an organization with discipline, communications, and transportation.

Using school children and large elements of the unemployed sector the army could restore the ecological integrity of the earth mother as a primary job. They could support and project large elements of society into the countryside.

When the day comes when a large combat force isn't needed to fight abroad then the alternatives to combat must be surfaced as intelligently thought out plans that can generate the enthusiasm of soldiers and members of the community alike.

Forests can be planted by children propelled to the site by army reserve or active units. These forests could be designed to effect weather patterns, enhance the beauty of the countryside with some interesting planting designs and even be used to make energy efficient pathways for aircraft over the deserts wherein the air is thin. Combining forests with new low energy waterway transportation and new canals would restore the supportive potential of the land to support the nation in an era of diminishing resources.
hark! it's the natural guard

THE FIRST EARTH BATTALION

ALAN ARMSTRONG IS THE AUTHOR OF THE SPIRAL FORREST. THE TREE PEOPLE OF L.A. HAVE PIONEERED MASS PLANTINGS USING SCHOOL CHILDREN.

one of mother Earth's pieces of super technology is the tree. Can you imagine tree paved pathways passing through the desert to give more lift to aircraft? Can you imagine what impact it would have if the children of egypt and israel planted a spiral forrest in the desert. It would provide an integrated border, eco consciousness and a visible reminder more striking than the great wall of china.

THE FIRST EARTH BATTALION

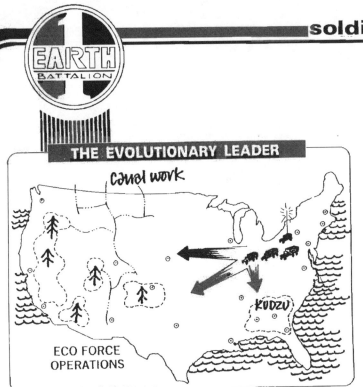

THE EVOLUTIONARY LEADER

canal work

ECO FORCE
OPERATIONS

KUDZU

<u>Eco force operations</u>

the manpower, communications organization and transport exist in todays military to transform the country-side.

Ask the military to spearhead a drive to replant the western desert areas...to connect the canals between Canada and the US. ...to harvest the kudzu in the southeast...and to make all their posts energy solvent by 1990.

they can do it!

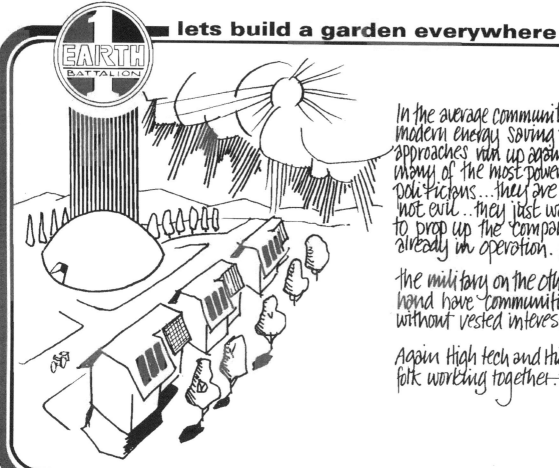

EARTH BATTALION 1

In the average community, modern energy saving approaches run up against many of the most powerful politicians...they are not evil...they just want to prop up the companies already in operation.

the military on the other hand have communities without vested interests.

Again High tech and High folk working together.

THE FIRST EARTH BATTALION

an EARTH BATTALION SUGGESTION:

the **ARMY** is a key element in the evolutionary jump about to occur. the National Guard will power the **ALPHA FORCE** in human rescue. the army reserve will catalize major evolutionary projects as the **BETA FORCE**. the active army will train and run the **GAMMA FORCE** as they operate strategically to resolve conflicts. the planning for evolutionary work and the attainment of paradise is already part of the army's **DELTA FORCE**.

military Organizations of the world have all been used to do evolutionary projects.

The American Army has been the leader in evolutionary work in this country:

- race integration
- computer revolution
- advanced schools
- social mobility
- rehabilitation
- sex integration
- systems revolution
- research & development

make them an offer they can't refuse!

THE FIRST EARTH BATTALION

there's lots to do.... what's your solution?

ALPHA FORCE | 1982 | NATURAL DISASTER RESCUE | BIO RESCUE | *The Natural Guard*
| | | NUCLEAR SURETY/RESCUE | ECO RESCUE |

BETA FORCE | 1982 | THE FREEDOM'S FORESTS PROJECT | *the Evolutionary Vanguard*
| | 1983 | THE SWEET SPOTS IN THE CITIES PROJECT |
| | 1984 | THE NEW HORIZON TOWNSHIPS PROJECT |

GAMMA FORCE *the Strategic Micro Force* | 1985 | THE WILDLIFE WATERWAYS PROJECT
| | 1986 | CONNECTIONS · NATIONAL TV PROJECT |

THE ACADEMY | 1987 | MUSIC IN THE WIND PROJECT

INTERNATIONAL TEAM | 1988 | COSMO CULTURE PROJECT

HOSTAGE INTERVENTION | **DELTA FORCE** | 1989 | GOOD WORKS PROJECT

TERRORIST INTERVENTION | | 1990 | ARTISTS IN ACTION

NUCLEAR DEFUSSION | *the FIRST EARTH BATTALION* | 1991 | RIGHT ACTION

THE FIRST EARTH BATTALION

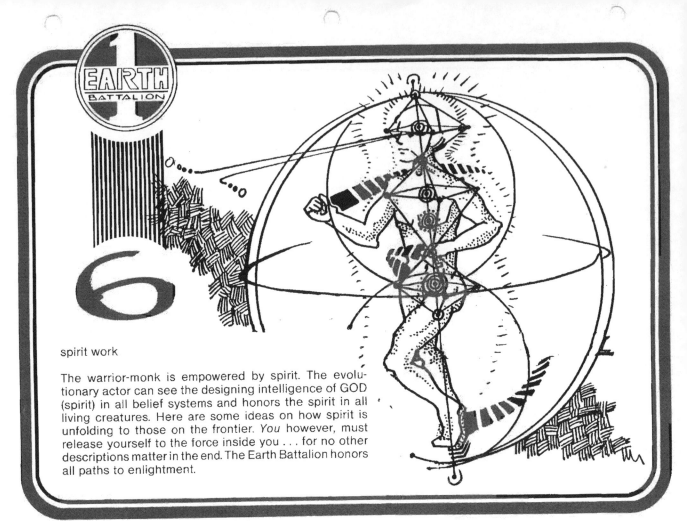

EARTH 1 BATTALION

6

spirit work

The warrior-monk is empowered by spirit. The evolutionary actor can see the designing intelligence of GOD (spirit) in all belief systems and honors the spirit in all living creatures. Here are some ideas on how spirit is unfolding to those on the frontier. *You* however, must release yourself to the force inside you . . . for no other descriptions matter in the end. The Earth Battalion honors all paths to enlightment.

THE FIRST EARTH BATTALION

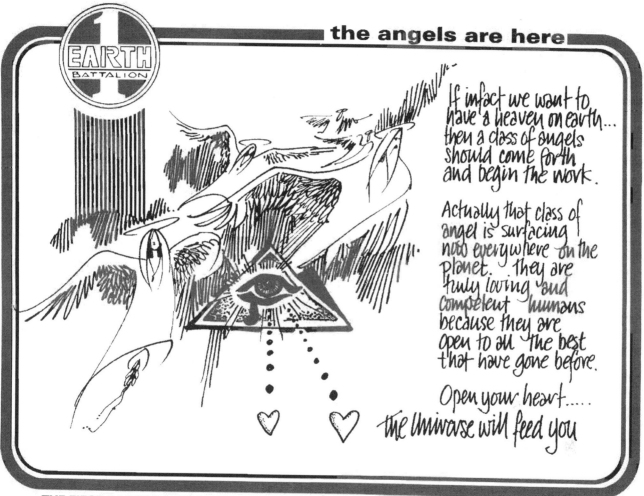

the angels are here

EARTH 1 BATTALION

If infact we want to have a heaven on earth... then a class of angels should come forth and begin the work.

Actually that class of angel is surfacing now everywhere on the planet... they are truly loving and competent humans because they are open to all the best that have gone before.

Open your heart.....
the Universe will feed you

THE FIRST EARTH BATTALION

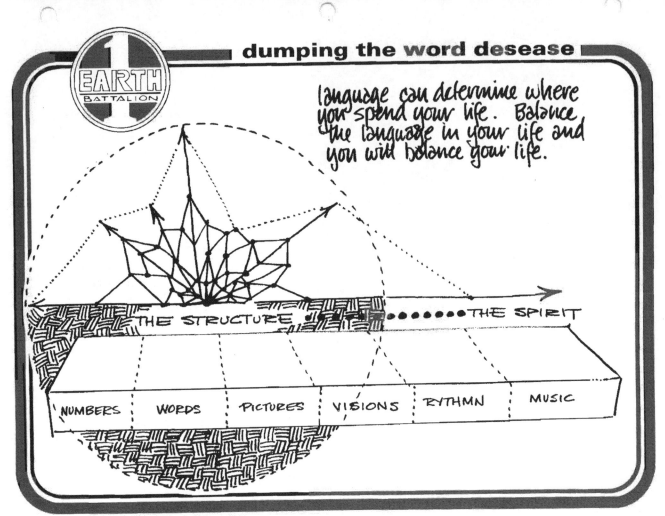

dumping the word desease

language can determine where you spend your life. Balance the language in your life and you will balance your life.

THE STRUCTURE ········· THE SPIRIT

NUMBERS | WORDS | PICTURES | VISIONS | RYTHMN | MUSIC

THE FIRST EARTH BATTALION

listen to the music

THE FIRST EARTH BATTALION

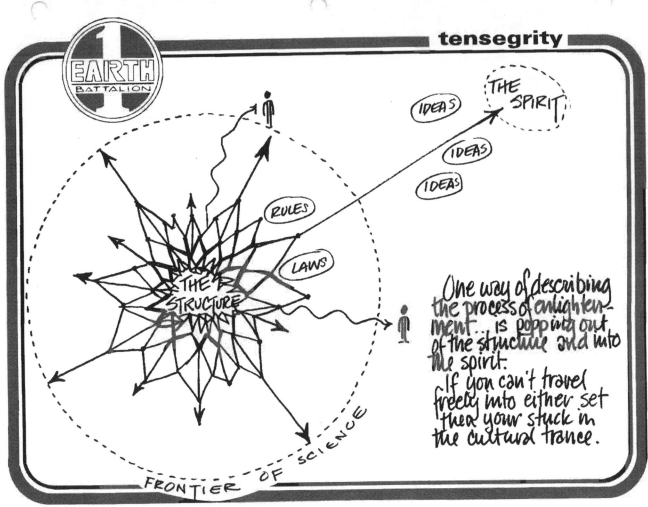

THE SPIRIT

IDEAS
IDEAS
IDEAS

RULES

LAWS

THE STRUCTURE

FRONTIER OF SCIENCE

One way of describing the process of enlightenment... is popping out of the structure and into the spirit.
If you can't travel freely into either set then your stuck in the cultural trance.

EARTH
1
BATTALION

THE FIRST EARTH BATTALION

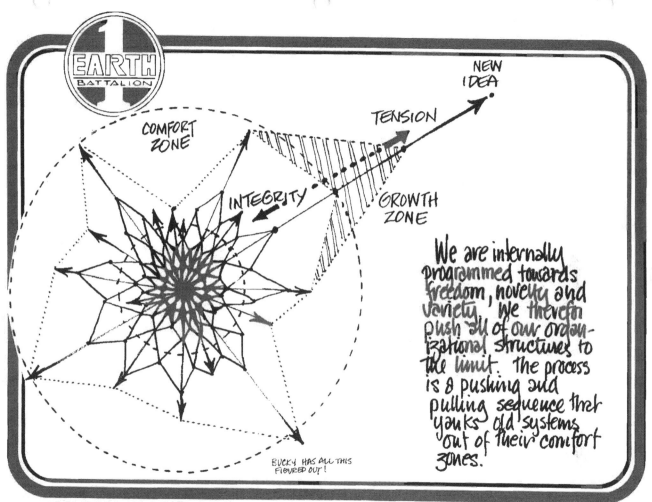

NEW IDEA

COMFORT ZONE

TENSION

INTEGRITY

GROWTH ZONE

We are internally programmed towards freedom, novelty and variety. We therefore push all of our organizational structures to the limit. The process is a pushing and pulling sequence that yanks old systems out of their comfort zones.

BUCKY HAS ALL THIS FIGURED OUT!

THE FIRST EARTH BATTALION

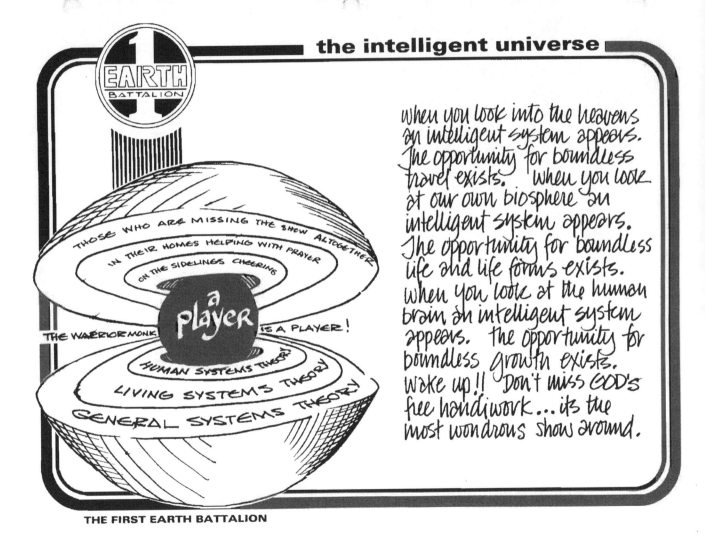

EARTH BATTALION 1

THOSE WHO ARE MISSING THE SHOW ALTOGETHER

IN THEIR HOMES HELPING WITH PRAYER

ON THE SIDELINES CHEERING

a player

THE WARRIOR MONK ... IS A PLAYER!

HUMAN SYSTEMS THEORY

LIVING SYSTEMS THEORY

GENERAL SYSTEMS THEORY

when you look into the heavens an intelligent system appears. The opportunity for boundless travel exists. When you look at our own biosphere an intelligent system appears. The opportunity for boundless life and life forms exists. When you look at the human brain an intelligent system appears. the opportunity for boundless growth exists. wake up!! Don't miss GOD's free handiwork... its the most wondrous show around.

THE FIRST EARTH BATTALION

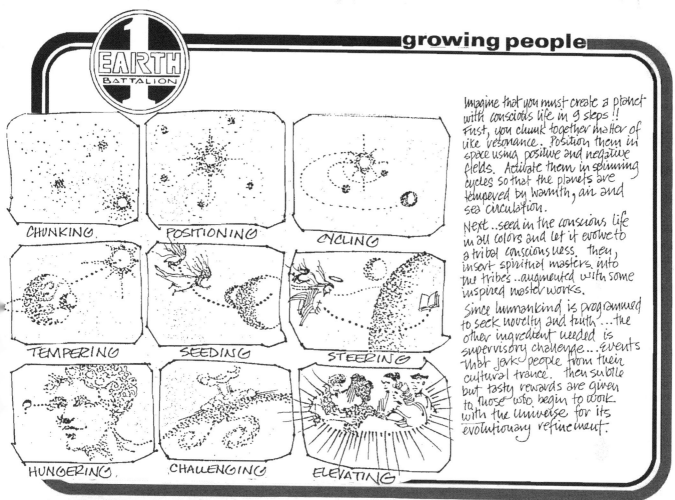

EARTH BATTALION 1

CHUNKING

POSITIONING

CYCLING

TEMPERING

SEEDING

STEERING

HUNGERING

CHALLENGING

ELEVATING

Imagine that you must create a planet with conscious life in 9 steps!!
First, you chunk together matter of like resonance. Position them in space using positive and negative fields. Activate them in spinning cycles so that the planets are tempered by warmth, air and sea circulation.

Next..seed in the conscious life in all colors and let it evolve to a tribal consciousness. then, insert spiritual masters into the tribes..augmented with some inspired master works.

Since humankind is programmed to seek novelty and truth...the other ingredient needed is supervisory challenge...events that jerk people from their cultural trance. then subtle but tasty rewards are given to those who begin to work with the universe for its evolutionary refinement.

THE FIRST EARTH BATTALION

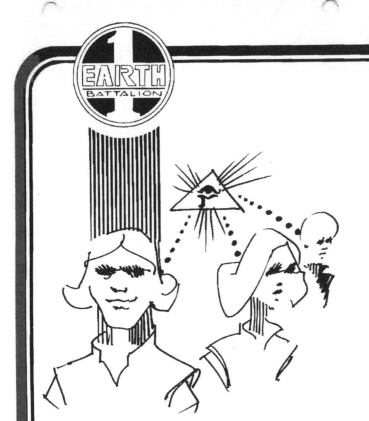

god is....and god becomes.

Evolution is what's happening to the universe and therefore evolution is god as a verb.

Evolution is our choice over stagnation or devolution.

Evolution is god's promise to be and to become god. The matter, energy, information and life forms that comprise the is...are designed in such a way to cooperate with evolution.

we are all ONE as god.
we can be evolution (but you must choose)

THE FIRST EARTH BATTALION

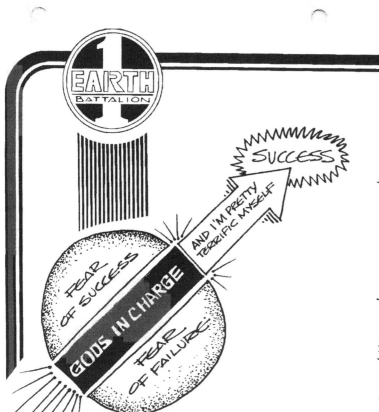

1 EARTH BATTALION

FEAR OF SUCCESS

FEAR OF FAILURE

GODS IN CHARGE

AND I'M PRETTY TERRIFIC MYSELF

SUCCESS

IMPORTANT FOOTNOTE: GOD IS WITHIN EACH OF US.

Evidence abounds that people who think they're OK just turn out to be OK. Those who fear they may fail will be too conservative to take chances... and those who fear they might succeed and are unsure of what that means... will never commit themselves totally. But those who realize they ARE PRETTY TERRIFIC and that GODS IN CHARGE anyway... can take off full steam to the top... without a worry.

THE FIRST EARTH BATTALION

THE UNIVERSE WORKS THE WAY ITS SUPPOSED TO ... RIGHT NOW.

THE UNIVERSE HAS NO AXES TO GRIND.

THE UNIVERSE SOMETIMES WORKS BEST WHEN ITS GIVING YOU A ROUGH TIME.

THE UNIVERSE HAS BIASED HUMANS TOWARD FREEDOM, NOVELTY & VARIETY.

HUMANS ARE AND BECOME JUST WHAT THEY PICTURE THEY ARE AND BECOME.

HUMANS GET WHAT THEY NEED.

HUMANS CAN BECOME ENLIGHTENED NOW OR LATER ... THE UNIVERSE HAS TIME.

SINCE THE UNIVERSE PAYS OFF DIRECTLY WHEN YOU WORK FOR PEOPLE AND PLANET ... WE HAVE NO CHOICE but to be wonderful!

THE FIRST EARTH BATTALION

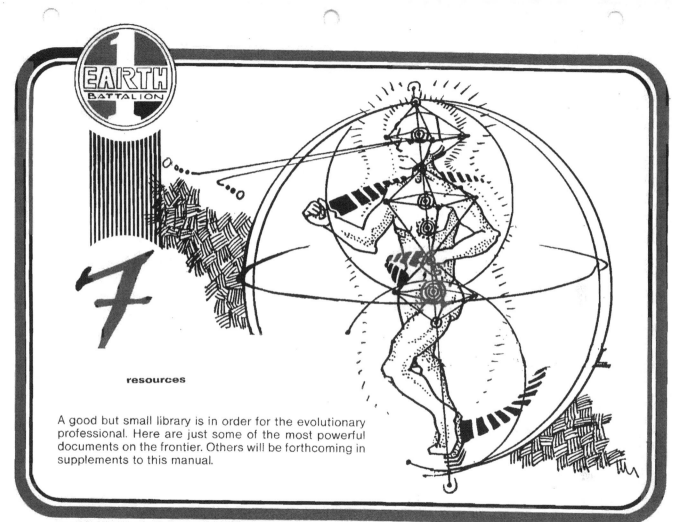

EARTH 1 BATTALION

7

resources

A good but small library is in order for the evolutionary professional. Here are just some of the most powerful documents on the frontier. Others will be forthcoming in supplements to this manual.

THE FIRST EARTH BATTALION

EARTH 1 BATTALION

for starters _____

OUR PAST IS NOT OUR POTENTIAL.

THE AQUARIAN CONSPIRACY by Marilyn Ferguson

| Hardcover edition | $15.00 |
| Softcover edition | 7.95 |

There are many new and exciting resources to assist your team with their personal evolution. Some are written and some are packaged trainings. Depending on whether you have access to a large enough city to do any of the trainings you can choose the written offerings instead. Many of the books must also be purchased in alternative bookstores in relatively large cities. For that reason we have included a larger number of works, many of which should be locally available.

The trainings are all only as effective as the particular trainers you draw. Never-the-less, the trainings we have selected have a national reputation generally worthy of good quality control.

The *URANTIA BOOK* and *COURSE IN MIRACLES* can nicely support weekly discussions. Many of the rest of the books are best used for individual work.

THE FIRST EARTH BATTALION

EARTH BATTALION 1

reading for background

Bibliography

THE MOST EXTENSIVE BIBLIOGRAPHY I KNOW IS IN:
THE BOOK OF HIGHS by EDWARD ROSENFELD © 1973
by quadrangle / New York Times Book Co.

Teilhard de Chardin, Pierre. *The Future of Man.* New York: Harper & Row, 1969.

Teilhard de Chardin, Pierre. *The Phenomenon of Man.* New York: Harper & Row, 1959.

Whorf, Benjamin L. *Language, Thought and Reality.* Cambridge, Mass.: MIT, 1956.

Watts, Alan. *The Book: On the Taboo Against Knowing Who You Are.* New York: Collier, 1966.

Alpert, Richard (Baba Ram Dass) & The Lama Foundation. *Be Here Now.* New York: Crown, 1971.

Castaneda, Carlos. *Journey to Ixtlan.* New York: Simon & Schuster, 1972.

Castaneda, Carlos. *A Separate Reality.* New York: Simon & Schuster, 1971.

Castaneda, Carlos. *The Teachings of Don Juan.* New York: Ballantine, 1968.

Cheng, Man-ching, & Smith, Robert W. *Tai-Chi.* Rutland, Vt., 1966.

DeRopp, Robert S. *The Master Game.* New York: Delta, 1968.

Ehrets, Arnold. *A Guide to Rational Fasting.* New York: Lustrum, 1972.

Hall, Edward T. *The Silent Language.* New York: Fawcett, 1959.

Lilly, John C. *Programming and Metaprogramming in the Human Biocomputer: Theory and Experiments.* New York: Julian, 1972.

Lilly, John C. *The Center of the Cyclone.* New York: Julian, 1972.

Masters, Robert E. L., & Houston, Jean. *New Ways of Being.* New York: Viking. In press.

Ouspensky, P. D. *The Fourth Way.* New York: Knopf, 1959.

THE FIRST EARTH BATTALION

there are other needs....

and there are plans for other alternative forces.

they will include the old and the young.

guided mythology

THE FIRST EARTH BATTALION

the First Earth Battalion
Foundation (north)
114 6th street
Steilacoom, Wa. 98388

THE FIRST EARTH BATTALION

be nice to your mother

Thanks friends

THIS INFORMATION HAS BEEN COLLECTED BY DIRECT EXPERIENCE WITH THE
TRAINERS OR TRAINING MATERIALS CREATED BY OVER 150 NEWAGE GROUPS,
FUTURISTS, PSYCHOTHERAPISTS, THEOLOGIANS, MARTIAL ARTS MASTERS AND A
WIDE ARRAY OF PRACTITIONERS BOTH WESTERN AND EASTERN, ANCIENT AND
MODERN, AND ORTHODOX AND MYSTIC HAVE GENERATED THESE PRACTICAL
RESPONSES TO THE CALL FOR A NEW AGE FOR HUMANKIND. SPECIAL THANKS
IS DUE MARILYN FERGESON, LTC FRANK BURNS, OSCAR ICHASO, COL MIKE
MALONE, BILL HARVEY, LTC JOHN ALEXANDER, BARBARA MARX HUBBARD, LTC
FRANK AKERS, BEA MILLER, JOHN ROGER, OLE NYDAL, GEORGE LEONARD, JOHN
DAVIDSON, BILL HELM, PATRICK WATSON, BOB AND LIA KLAUS, LTC BILL WITT,
SGT D, SHELA RUMACK, LTC DENNIS FOLEY, ALAN ARMSTRONG, CAROLYN MYSS,
DR. JERRY EPPLER, COL HOWARD PRINCE, THE DELTA FORCE TEAM, TERRY
DOBSON, THE PACIFIC INSTITUTE, RON MEDVED, THE URANTIA BROTHERHOOD,
MICHAEL NEBADON, GRANT RAMEY, THE CENTER OF THE FORM, NANCY GROSSMAN,
COL TONY POKORNEY, LTG LEE, LAWRIE DEBIVORT, BART BOYCE, ALAN GIBB,
JOE MILLER, JOHN MC NEIL, HELEN AND GEORGE BESCH, A HALF A DOZEN
EASTERN GURU'S AND VARIOUS OTHER FOLKS OF QUESTIONABLE ORIGIN.
SPECIAL THANKS TO MY FAMILY RITA, PARKER AND BROOKE WHO FROM TIME
TO TIME PROBABLY QUESTION MY ORIGIN.

Home

FOR ONE OF THESE WRITE ILLUMINATIONS BOX 1000 CAMBRIDGE, MA. 02139

Jim Channon
LTC. U.S. ARMY

SPECIAL THANKS TO:

LISETTE MEYER ... LAYOUT
CAROL HOSS ... PAINTINGS
ANDERS H. .... FLAGS
GARY ALLEN ... CONCEPTS
JONATHAN ... MUSIC
CHRISTIAN · MARILYN ... PRINTING
LOU TICE ... SUPPORT

THE FIRST EARTH BATTALION

barriers: identify traditional thought forms or expected behavior that is simply no longer useful or empowering to your development in this area.

memory check: describe what memory jogger you will use and where you will put it to remind you to do the visualization.

projected picture of success/action: describe how you will see yourself actually being successful in realizing this challenge.

journal item: record here life events that resulted from your visualization.

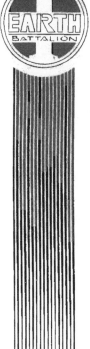

FIRST EARTH BATTALION

FIRST EARTH BATTALION

LTC JIM CHANNON
GARY W. ALLEN
114 · 6TH ST   584-9173
STEILACOOM, WA   98388

home base ↑

your card ↑

audio-cassette label ↑ (coming soon)

EARTH BATTALION CUT OUTS

FIRST EARTH BATTALION

your notepad ↓

THE NATURAL GUARD

I envision an international ideal of service awakening in an emerging class of people who are best called *evolutionaries*. I see them as soldiers, as youth, and as those who have soldier spirit within them. I see them come together in the name of *people* and *planet* to create a new environment of support for the positive growth of humankind and the living earth mother. Their mission is to protect the possible and nurture the potential. They are the evolutionary guardians who focus their loving protection and affirm their allegiance to people and planet for their own good and for the good of those they serve. I call them *evolutionaries*, not *revolutionaries*, for they are potentialists, not pragmatists. They are pioneers, not palace guards.

Dear Friend:

Your initial requests for information caught us by surprise. We were not staffed to handle individual requests but fortunately now have a splendid illustrated manual/mini-course that explains the *First Earth Battalion* in the best possible way. In addition you can have the best synthesis of the new and powerful techniques available to increase your own power to grow and have a positive impact on the world around you.

-SURVEY-

Check the blocks below and help us determine other items you might be interested in in the future.

SURVEY ONLY—NOT AN ORDER FORM

☐ Would you be interested in a quality T-shirt "Iron On" at $5.00?

☐ Would you be interested in a 3-ring binder to build your personal journal and collect manual pages at $5.00?

☐ Would you be interested in an antenna flag (14x28") in bright nylon at $25.00 a piece?

☐ Other _____

SURVEY FORM

CUT ALONG THIS LINE FOR ORDER FORM

Dear Earth Battalion,

Please mail ____ copy(ies) of the "Evolutionary Tactics" manual and mini-course at the first edition price of $12.50 per manual.

I have passed the attached cards to ____ other evolutionary friends who may want to participate in this first edition offer.

Please send the copy(ies) to these address(es)

PLEASE MAKE CHECKS PAYABLE TO FIRST EARTH BN FOUNDATION   Allow 30 days for handling and shipment.

THE FIRST EARTH BATTALION

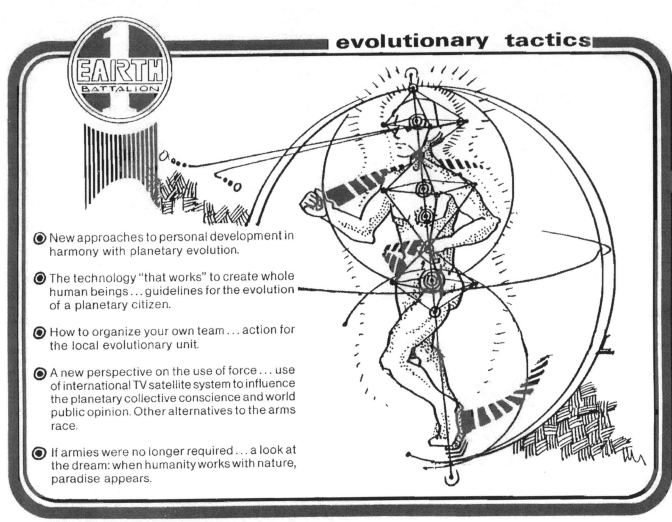

EARTH 1 BATTALION

- New approaches to personal development in harmony with planetary evolution.

- The technology "that works" to create whole human beings ... guidelines for the evolution of a planetary citizen.

- How to organize your own team ... action for the local evolutionary unit.

- A new perspective on the use of force ... use of international TV satellite system to influence the planetary collective conscience and world public opinion. Other alternatives to the arms race.

- If armies were no longer required ... a look at the dream: when humanity works with nature, paradise appears.

THE FIRST EARTH BATTALION

CLIP THESE OUT AND GIVE THEM
TO YOUR IDEALISTIC FRIENDS
↓

SEND CHECK FOR $12.50 TO FIRST EARTH BATTALION FOUNDATION.

SEND CHECK FOR $12.50 TO FIRST EARTH BATTALION FOUNDATION.

SEND CHECK FOR $12.50 TO FIRST EARTH BATTALION FOUNDATION.

The earth battalion declares its primary allegiance to **people** and **planet.** You can become a part of that allegiance right where you are simply by allowing the exquisite human being inside to come out. When it's out... help others to come out and then work together cooperatively to stay out — building the paradise that is possible when we cooperate with each other and our mother the earth.

THE FIRST EARTH BATTALION

114 - 6TH ST
STEILACOOM, WA 98388

"... my allegiance goes beyond duty, honor and country ... to PEOPLE and PLANET."

LTC. JIM CHANNON, US ARMY

Not all people have the courage to take charge of themselves. But everyone has enough warrior and enough monk inside to become a powerful and yet sensitive evolutionary. This manual is designed to connect you with your own power to act.

The concept designer, author and illustrator is Lieutenant Colonel Jim Channon, a professional soldier. His military training gives operational focus to new age concepts.

dare to think the unthinkable
a network of evolutionary activists has developed a positive doctrine to allow people to take charge of their destiny again. People are the ultimate technology and the EARTH is our home.

THE FIRST EARTH BATTALION

74290671R00083

Made in the USA
Middletown, DE
22 May 2018